Our Lady's Apron

A collection of articles on spiritual topics

To Brian & Patricia

with best wishes

Fr. Christopher Fox, M.H.M.

Christopher Fox

Contents

INTRODUCTION

Over the years I have contributed articles to various religious magazines, Friends have suggested that these should be collected and published in book form. I have selected a number of them for publication here. I hope you find them helpful in developing your own relationship with God. We all approach God in our own personal way but it is well to keep in mind some essential truths, namely that the God we worship is a God of infinite love, made visible in the person of Our Saviour Jesus Christ. Each one of us is a unique human being, created in the image and likeness of God, a beloved daughter or son of a loving Father. Prayer in its widest definition is how we express our relationship with God.

That relationship is expressed in various ways, firstly by the life we live, a life of integrity and goodness, guided by the commandments and the precepts of the Gospel. No amount of devotional practices can compensate for lack of integrity in my daily life. Secondly we are called to worship God publicly. We do so in different ways guided by cultural norms and practices. For Catholics the supreme act of worship is the sacrifice of the Mass. Some of the articles focus on our understanding of the Eucharist. Thirdly for any relationship to grow, it needs time for intimate conversation. Time spent in private prayer is important for all of us and enriches our lives. We can talk and listen to God who will guide our faltering steps on our pilgrim journey through life.

In the following articles I have dealt with these and other matters. One can only regret the creeping materialism of modern life where spiritual matters are crowded out. A deep faith in a personal God is a sure foundation for happiness. I pray that the enclosed articles may help in some way to confirm that faith.

I have chosen for my title *Our Lady's Apron*. When I was a young lad growing up in rural Ireland many of the countrywomen wore a large apron made from canvas or hessian or perhaps checked calico. It was primarily a protective garment but when the two lower corners were gathered together it became a convenient receptacle for carrying a head of cabbage, potatoes, eggs or maybe a frail newborn lamb or whatever the exigencies of the farmyard dictated.

I now humbly implore the Blessed Virgin Mary to gather my few writings into her apron and carry them to her Son for his approval and blessing and I fervently pray that all who read these words may be enfolded in that blessing.

Fr. Christopher Fox.

OUR SEARCH FOR MEANING IN LIFE

I search and seek I know not what.
I only know it must be there.
For in my heart there is a quest
For something more than earth lays bare.

For even in the midst of bliss
Or what for bliss does falsely pass,
I know there's something hid from me,
Some truth beyond this earthly mass.

And so I delve and probe and sift
The sands on this our exile shore
To find that dim elusive truth
That stands when time shall be no more.

This poem expresses the quest for meaning and love that is rooted in every human heart. The deepest search in life is not for power or pleasure. It is a search for meaning and love. Genuine religion tries to provide a key to that search, the acknowledgement of a Supreme Being, the source and origin of all life, to Whom we owe love and obedience. I see our Christian religion as providing the most beautiful key of all to understanding the meaning of life and love. However not everybody sees it this way.

In our modern world it is fashionable to look upon people with strong religious beliefs as somewhat eccentric at best, out of touch with our brave new world, and at worst, just plain dumb, unworthy of a hearing. One gets this attitude from some columnists in our newspapers, from some book reviewers and panellists on chat shows. Some of these people can have a very prejudiced view of religion often citing distortions of religious practice rather than looking at the real doctrine. Some of their comments are unworthy of a serious critic.

While I respect people who after due consideration have come to a form of agnosticism or atheism, and there are serious arguments in that direction, it seems to me that even on an intellectual level there are much stronger arguments for belief in God. The beliefs of the vast majority of human beings cannot be dismissed at pure superstition.

The strangest idea of all is the curious assumption that to close the door on religion is to step into a wider world. Tell me, if you wish as Richard Dawkins does, that my beliefs are all delusions, but please don't tell me that my vision of human life stretching beyond time and space is smaller than one which sees it ending as a handful of dust.

The late Fr. John Harriott, S.J., a gifted columnist, put it very succinctly, "To believe that human beings are infinitely precious to God, reflect His nature which they are born to share and by grace can stretch their powers beyond their natural reach, is surely infinitely more enriching than to think of them as animate slime". Delusion it may be but at least it is a delusion of grandeur, adding point and energy and nobility to life. And to reject it, if you must, is hardly a matter for self-congratulation, but rather of mourning and the drawing down of the blinds."

To reject religion may be honest for some but it is not exactly leaping a prison wall into freedom. It is more like jumping into a dustbin, not a grand illusion, more a putting out of the lights. To focus only on the faults of distorted religion and some absurd religious practices and to look no further is not the mark of a superior mind but more an indication of grave prejudice.

Religion has captured and inspired some of the greatest minds the world has ever known and will continue to do so. I thank God each day of my life for my Christian faith, which has strengthened and motivated me in good times and in bad. I also thank God for my missionary vocation which gave me the opportunity to share that faith with people of different cultures and backgrounds. It has been a great source of courage and happiness to me during a very eventful life. There is a quote from St. Paul, which I like to use frequently: *"To me this grace was given, to preach to the peoples the unsearchable riches of Christ."*

Isn't it strange that princes and kings
And clowns that caper in sawdust rings
And ordinary folk like you and me
Are builders of eternity?

To each is given a bag of tools,
An hourglass and a book of rules,
And each must build 'ere time is flown
A stumbling block or a stepping stone

Anon

WHAT IS PRAYER?

There's a story about the late Monsignor Ronald Knox meeting an acquaintance one Sunday morning while on his way to say Mass. His friend was carrying a bulging golf bag. In response to the Monsignor's gentle reproving gesture, the man said cheerfully, "Don't worry, Monsignor, I can pray just as well on the golf course as you do in church." Knox, with typical sharp wit, said, "Oh really, and do you?"

A good question because prayer, a lifting of the mind and heart to God, is essentially a practical subject rather than a theoretical one. Prayer is a pathway which one makes by walking on it. True, there are many excellent books on prayer which can be very helpful. But it's a bit like learning how to drive a car. You never really know much until you sit behind the wheel and learn by experience. The first rule of prayer is: do it. Spend some time at it and learn by experience. Another good guideline is: pray as you can, not as you can't. Choose a form of prayer which suits your temperament and lifestyle. Choose a suitable time and place. But do give some time to it. As the saying goes, if you are too busy to pray, then you are too busy.

The past few years have seen a collapse of accepted patterns of prayer and devotions in our homes and parishes. Yet deep down in us there is a hunger for spiritual values, a search for ways to get in touch with our deeper selves, to have some experience of a loving God.

There are many definitions of prayer. The old one that it is a raising of the mind and heart to God is still very valid. There are others which are complimentary to that. Prayer is talking and listening to God, listening and learning, learning and doing. It is a search for integrity in my life, allowing God to help me discern His will and to conduct my life accordingly. It is impossible to continue an unChristian form of attitude or action with deep prayer which allows God to speak to the heart. God will show us where we must change.

My favourite definition of prayer is, a loving awareness of God in my life. The foundation of all prayer is a personal faith in a loving God. That loving awareness has to sink from the head to the heart. The spiritual writer, Fr. Dalrymple, entitled one of his books *The Longest Journey*, the journey from the head to the heart.

I remember the late Cardinal Heenan in an interview with David Frost was thrown the question, "For you, what's the hardest Christian concept to accept?" Heenan didn't speak of the Blessed Trinity or the Incarnation. He simply said, "I suppose the fact that God loves me." He was touching on the incredible mystery at the heart of our Christian faith, that each one of us for all our imperfections and sinfulness is precious and lovable in the eyes of the Creator.

A deep awareness of a loving God is the starting point of all prayer. My relationship with God should be expressed in three ways. Firstly by living a life of honesty and goodness according to the Christian commandments. No amount of prayer or devotion can compensate for lack of integrity in my life. Secondly we are called upon to worship God publicly as a community. The highest form of worship for us Catholics is the

Sacrifice of the Mass. This is the celebration of our identity as disciples of Christ. Lastly any love relationship requires time spent alone with the beloved. This is what private prayer is all about when we go into the room of our heart to experience God's loving presence. There we can express our feelings of love and adoration, of sorrow for sin, of thanksgiving for graces received and we can tell God all our needs.

Prayers of intercession are a most common form of prayer. Jesus himself once told his disciples, *"Ask and it will be given to you; seek and you will find; knock and the door will be opened to you. For the one who asks always receives; the one who seeks always finds and the one who knocks will always have the door opened".*
(Matt. 7: 7-12)

However this form of prayer does raise questions. Will God work miracles in answer to my prayers. Perhaps. In the Acts of the Apostles, chapter 12, we read how Peter was miraculously freed from prison through the power of prayer. In the medical bureau at Lourdes I have seen clear records of some of the miraculous cures which happened at the Shrine. But these are extraordinary events. God usually works through more ordinary but yet impressive ways. For instance the vast majority of cures in Lourdes are in the area of spiritual healing, people receiving the grace of courage and resignation to accept God's will and to see one's suffering in a new light.

Every prayer contributes to the health of the Church, the Body of Christ. Every prayer poured out in faith and love in some way is channelled into a vast reservoir of merit from which countless people can draw to their health and healing. No prayer is ever lost. There are a few basic truths which we should keep in mind. When we pray for a safe journey we must not expect God to intervene if we take foolish risks. If we pray for peace we are really praying for the strength to work to create a climate of peace. The bottom line of all our prayers is to discern and do God's holy will.

Every prayer is answered but perhaps not in the way we expected. God sees our real needs which may differ from what we pray for and the answer is always for our benefit and the glory of God. This is summed up beautifully in a little poem by Henry Viscardi.

> I asked for riches that I might be happy.
>   I was given poverty that I might be wise.
> I asked for power that I might have the praise of men.
>   I was given weakness that I might feel the need of God.
> I asked for all things that I might enjoy life.
>   I was given life that I might enjoy all things.
> I got nothing that I asked for, but everything that I hoped for,
>   Almost despite myself my unspoken prayers were answered.
> I am, among all men, most richly blessed.

PRAYER AT A TIME OF TRAGEDY

I was in New York on the morning of the eleventh of September, 2001, known widely as 9/11, when the twin towers were destroyed by suicide bombers using planes as their weapons. I had arrived the night before to officiate at the wedding of my nephew, Kevin, the following Saturday. The atrocity of 9/11 is indelibly etched on all our memories. It was felt all over the world but to be on the spot, to see the devastation right near you, to watch the collapsing towers and the falling bodies is something I will always recall with horror. I remember going back to the church where I had said Mass that morning and spending the afternoon in prayer. Why, O Lord, why? People were asking, Where was God in all this?

I could only reflect that God, Emmanuel, was right there with the firemen, the police, the nurses and doctors and the countless ordinary men and women who rose to the occasion, performing heroic acts of self-sacrifice and courage to bring life and hope to others. Jesus, Emmanuel, while being crucified again with the victims of atrocity was also there inspiring others to courage and love.

The following morning the churches were packed with worshippers. Many felt that prayer was the only answer they could give, prayer of reparation for the evil done, prayer for the eternal repose of the victims who had perished – a neighbouring parish lost 37 of its members, many of them firemen – prayers of petition for courage and wisdom to see one's way through the awful tragedy.

Two evenings later I was one of a vast crowd at a candle-lit service in a nearby park. It was very moving. At the end I noticed that someone had placed a large placard under the huge pole hoisting the American flag. Written on it was a quote from Bl. Mother Teresa of Calcutta:

> *The fruit of silence is prayer,*
> *The fruit of prayer is faith.*
> *The fruit of faith is love.*
> *The fruit of love is service.*
> *The fruit of service is peace.*

I felt the quote brought out the essential aspect of genuine religion, prayer nourishing a deep personal faith in a loving God, prayer issuing forth in love and service and bringing peace to our troubled world. It is the response that is needed especially when things go wrong. God speaks to us through all the events of our lives. We need to reflect deeply and try to discern what the message is and what is the appropriate response.

Images play a powerful part in the way we worship God. Two great obstacles to growth in genuine prayer are a poor self-image and a poor God image. Some forms of Catholic piety tended to create a poor self-image in us, some preachers insisting that we are all miserable sinners. That is wrong. While we are all aware of our weaknesses, our failures, we must also be aware of our unique dignity as children of God. At the baptism of Jesus, the Father's voice is heard, *"This is my beloved Son"*. By our baptism we are born into the body of Christ, the Church. Each one of us by our birthright has the right to hear the Father say to us. "This is my beloved son, this is my beloved daughter." We need to let that incredible truth sink into our deep consciousness. Whatever our limitations are, we can still walk tall. We are brothers and sisters of Jesus; we are beloved children of a loving God. We dare to say Abba, Father.

The second obstacle to spiritual maturity is a poor God-image. One of the saddest scenes we witnessed on our TV screens after 9/11 was the sight of the followers of Bin Laden, some of them children, gloating over the massacre and crying "Allah is great." If that is their image of God, who wants such a God, a monster? We must not forget that down the centuries terrible things have been done in the name of God by people professing the Christian faith. Someone once said, that nothing hides the face of God as much as religion, meaning religion distorted by prejudice, hatred and bigotry.

We are challenged to ask of ourselves what image of God do I have in my mind when I pray. Faulty preaching in the past on hellfire and damnation didn't help. Some people kept the resulting scars and guilt-feelings till their dying day. Some obeyed out of fear rather than out of love. Awe and reverence are at the heart of religious worship but the essence of the Good News is LOVE, a love embodied in the person of Jesus. We read in John 3:16 *"For God loved the world so much that He gave His only Son so that everyone who believes in Him may not be lost but may have eternal life."*

We will always have a very limited image of the infinite God, but the only sure guide for each of us in forming that image is the Jesus portrayed in the Gospels. He is the visible face of the invisible God. He is God's fingerprints on our human flesh. He is God's self-portrait. For a healthy God image and real progress in prayer we should read and pray the Gospels.

No doubt religion has to answer for
some of the most terrible crimes in history.
But that is not the fault of religion
but of the ungovernable brute in man.

Mahatma Gandhi.

SPIRITUAL MATURITY THROUGH INVOCATION OF THE HOLY SPIRIT

"Yes, we can" was a recent political slogan. There is a very positive ring about it which we all need in our search for improvement whether physical, emotional or spiritual. We all want to grow a little in our relationships with God and our neighbour. That's why we read such articles as this one. However, most of us are more aware of our inadequacies than of our giftedness.

I often recommend three steps in developing personal spiritual maturity. They are

1. self-knowledge
2. self-acceptance
3. openness to the power of the Holy Spirit.

Let me explain these steps.

Self-knowledge is the start of any real growth in maturity. It was the axiom of the great philosopher Socrates: Know thyself. The most basic way to self-knowledge is to reflect deeply on one's life's experiences, how we faced the ups and downs of each day, our reaction to opportunities and challenges, how we related to others and how we coped with difficulties. This can be done is quiet reflective prayer towards the end of the day. If we have a friend who knows us well and reflects back to us his/her assessments honestly, even confronts us at times when we are going astray, then we are truly blessed. Great works of literature are sources of self-knowledge as they hold up a mirror to human nature in all its strengths and weaknesses. Shakespeare was one of the greatest psychologists that ever lived. He had an amazing insight into the human character and what makes people tick. More recently some people attend courses such as the Enneagram or the Myres Briggs Typology Indicator. They deal with the wonderful variety and complexity of the human personality. Many have found them a great help to self-understanding.

The second step, self-acceptance, is not quite as simple as it seems because we are all masters of self-denial in one way or another. A classic case is the alcoholic, who despite all the evidence, continues to deny that he/she has a problem. Sadly many people guilty of child abuse can go into total denial. Only when one reaches the stage of self-acceptance, "yes I have a problem" can treatment begin.

It may be difficult for many of us to accept ourselves as we are and to admit our failings: Yes, I have a short temper. Yes, I do bear a grudge and I cannot forgive that past hurt. Yes, I do spend too much time watching T.V. or indulging in idle gossip. Yes, I do complain too much. It's always difficult to accept our own failures and limitations. The great Cistercian spiritual writer, Thomas Merton, sums it up in his own humorous way when he said: "We take a great step in spiritual maturity the day we can accept that we'll never be a saint and we'll never be the Abbott."

When we honestly accept ourselves as we are with all our

limitations and inadequacies, then we need to take the third step rather than being daunted by our failures. **This most important step is to open our minds and hearts to the power of the Holy Spirit.** An old professor often reminded us that the Good News of the Gospel is not: "Try and you will succeed." It is "ASK AND YOU WILL RECEIVE." Invocation was one of the key words at the Second Vatican Council. We can invoke the power of the Holy Spirit at all times, which is the power of the Risen Christ dwelling within us. If one finds it hard to forgive a past hurt; ask for that grace to forgive. If one feels daunted by the challenges ahead, just ask for the courage required. Jesus has promised to be with us always.

It is so important to have a positive approach to life. The glass can be half full or half empty. To me it is always half-full. Every crisis is an opportunity for growth. See the positive in any situation. One of my favourite quotes from St. Paul is: Phil. 4: 8-9: "*...fill your minds with everything that is true, everything that is noble, everything that is good and pure, everything that we love and honour and everything that can be thought virtuous or worthy of praise... Then the God of Peace will be with you.*" A deep abiding trust in a loving personal God revealed in Jesus Christ is part of our Christian heritage. That trust is based not on our own great strength but on the power of the Risen Christ. With the grace of the Holy Spirit, yes we can.

There is a lovely story of **St. Francis of Assisi** and the leper. At the beginning of his conversion, he was still living with his wealthy father and was still very fastidious, with a natural aversion to anything unsightly or unpleasant. Out riding one day he came across a leper. His whole instinct was not to stop, just throw him a few coins and go on. Then he remembered the

Gospel. He stopped and dismounted. The leper held out his hand for a coin. Francis gave him what money he had and then embraced and kissed him. In doing so Francis embraced three lepers on that road.

a) The actual leper whose appearance first filled him with horror.

b) The dark side of his own personality. This pleasure loving young man was very uncomfortable in the face of ugliness or stench. Now he faced up to this fact and embraced his own dark shadow, his weakness, his sinfulness.

c) He embraced the person of Christ who accepted our humanity with all its frailty in order to bring us salvation. On that day, Francis became a true disciple of Christ and began his heroic mission in the Church.

WE DARE TO SAY: ABBA, FATHER.

Every genuine Christian longs to grow in intimacy with God. The way to do so is through a deep personal prayer life. Jesus in his public ministry led a very active life but what often impressed his disciples was the number of occasions when he took time out to be alone with His Father. Mark's Gospel details the hectic activity of the ministry of Jesus, yet Mark includes significant mention of these occasions.

"In the morning long before dawn he got up and left the house and went off to a lonely place and prayed there" (Mk.1:35). We should see these references as part of the Good News Mark wished to hand on to us, namely, that whatever our pre-occupations or demands, we need to take time out for private prayer, to be alone with God. This time given to God will enrich all our other activities.

On one occasion a disciple asked: " Lord teach us to pray." In response, Jesus gave us the *Our Father.* The wording is found in both Matthew and Luke, slightly different, but basically the same. We are most familiar with Matthew's version. (Matt. 6: 9-16). It is one of the first prayers we learned but it is possible that saying it by rote so often, the full impact of the words can be lost on us.   We need at times to pause and reflect deeply on their meaning.

The *Our Father* is our religious anthem. It is a summary of the Gospels. It is the prayer of Christian identity, because it expresses the essence of divine revelation brought to us by Jesus. From the very beginning it was central to the prayer of the Church. In the celebration of the Eucharist it links the great prayer of consecration with the sacred banquet of Holy Communion.

Some of the great saints wrote extensively on this prayer. St. Thomas Aquinas called it the perfect prayer because in it we ask for all the things we can rightly desire and in the right order. St. Teresa of Avila, when once asked how to become a contemplative, simply advised the person to reflect on the Our Father each day for one hour. St. Catherine of Sienna seldom finished the prayer as she was so caught up in one or other of the magnificent petitions.

It begins with the words *Our Father*. This reveals God's relationship with us as that of a caring loving parent. In the Old Testament God is often seen as the Almighty One, the Creator, the stern judge, remote and fearsome. Some preachers in the past stressed that image too much. Two great obstacles to growth in spiritual maturity are a poor God image and a poor self image. Jesus reveals the real image of God. "To those who did accept Him, he gave power to become children of God" (Jn.1:12). St. Paul in his letter to the Romans is very emphatic: "The spirit you received is not the spirit of slaves bringing fear into your lives; it is the spirit of sons and it makes us cry out Abba – Father." (Rom. 8:15) Again "God sent the Spirit of His Son into your hearts crying out Abba-Father." (Gal. 4:6).

The word Abba is used by Jesus in his prayer in the agony in the Garden of Gethsemane. *"Abba – Father, all things are possible for you. Take this cup away from me. Nevertheless, not what I will but what you will."* (Mark 14:36)

In most cultures children have an affectionate name for parents, often the first name they pronounce. For their fathers, it is usually: dada, papa, baba (China). It is a title of intimacy. The Aramaic word ABBA has this meaning. In our relationship with God it is important to acknowledge His greatness as Creator, the Almighty One, the Upholder of the universe, but this does not exclude the more intimate, beautiful, affectionate title as we dare to say Abba-Father. Abba expresses the closeness of a child for a loving parent. The more formal word, Father, conveys an intelligent understanding of our relationship to God in Jesus. The two combined show the fullness of our emotional attachment to and our intelligent understanding of our heavenly Father.

In the Our Father there are seven petitions. The first three are focussed directly on God, expressing adoration and praise and total submission to His will. The other four are concerned with our desire to live out our Christian commitment with our brothers and sisters as we try to make the Kingdom of God a reality in our lives. They provide an unlimited source of meditation for all of us. So if we find it hard to pray we can simply close our eyes and say the *Our Father* slowly, with devotion and love, and with as much concentration as we are capable of and realise that you are united with countless people round the world saying the beautiful prayer that Jesus taught us.

ON PRAYING BEFORE THE CRIB.

One of my earliest memories is being taken by my mother to Mullingar, the local market town, at Christmas. It was a big treat for a rural boy, seeing the decorated streets, the crowded shops, the town lights. The outing always included a visit to the Cathedral. I was probably more interested in the click of my new shoes on the steps leading up to the entrance and then the long walk down the central aisle, but my abiding memory is of my mother kneeling in silent prayer before the Crib.

The beautiful tableau, the Infant Jesus, His Blessed Mother, St Joseph standing guard, the angels, the shepherds, the hushed silence, all provided a great contrast to the hustle and bustle outside. Even for a young lad of six it was an experience of another world, a spiritual world, a world other than that of toys and football and school. I remember the stillness, the people kneeling and praying. Even before I knew much about prayer, I got the sense of a loving God being present there, touching our lives.

Praying before the Crib is part of our rich Catholic tradition. The Crib is simply a visible reminder of the great mystery of the Incarnation, the central tenet of our Christian faith. The Word became flesh and pitched His tent amongst us. The story of the birth of Jesus is told in two of the Gospels, that of Matthew and of Luke. Each writer tells it from his own perspective, not giving a reporter's account of literal facts but more a theological reflection on the great mystery. The Infancy narratives are not for a man with a measuring tape mind. Luke especially combines the mind of a theologian with the soul of a poet and produces a story of incomparable beauty.

It is claimed that Luke wrote the main part of his Gospel first and wrote the Infancy narrative last as a sort of overture to the great work which was about to unfold. In this overture he skilfully wove various themes which would be revealed in the main narrative. Thus the shepherds were the first to hear the good news of the Saviour's birth. Shepherds at the time were often the outcasts of society. This foreshadows the theme of Jesus's love for the poor and lowly which is so manifest in St. Luke's Gospel. The manger is a place of nourishment and can easily be seen as a symbol of Jesus as the Bread of Life, who nourishes us all in the Blessed Eucharist. *'No room in the Inn'* in many Nativity plays sees inn-keepers getting a rough time for rejecting Mary and Joseph in their hour of need. However, Luke would want us to see it in a different light. The inn in any village is a place where tourists and passing visitors stay. But if a member of my family comes, he or she will not be put up in the inn but must be accommodated in the heart of my home. Jesus did not come as a tourist or visitor to depart some time later. No, He came as a member of our family and would be born in the heart of our home, however lowly that home might be. He pitched His tent among us to remain with us forever.

As I kneel before the Crib I bow in humble adoration before the Christ Child. I think of the words of St. John's Gospel, *"God loved the world so much that He gave His Only Son so that everybody who believes in Him may have eternal life."* Christmas is a time for gifts so I kneel to thank God for the greatest gift of all, the gift of Jesus and the gift of my Christian faith.

I look at Mary and I pray for all mothers. I think of the sacrifices they make that their children may have life and I bless the memory of my own good mother. St. Joseph, the humble carpenter, stands quietly nearby, the protector of Jesus and Mary, and now named as the Protector of the Universal Church. I pray for his protection in these challenging times. I pray for all fathers. St. Joseph is often depicted as a senior figure. My own dad was 72 when I was born so my relationship with him was all the richer as I grew up. I think of all his values, his down-to-earth goodness and kindness, a very ordinary man but like so many other men and women of his generation who gave so much and were quietly heroic in their own way. I bless their memory.

Often my gaze wanders beyond the crib to the tabernacle on the altar, then further on to the cross above it. I ponder on the three incredible images God has put before us of His loving presence: that of a helpless baby in a manger, a piece of consecrated bread in the tabernacle and a helpless victim of violence nailed to a cross. What does it say to our contemporary world with its mad search for power, pleasure and celebrity status. If the rich and powerful could spend a few moments here before the Crib perhaps their values and priorities might change. Then I realise that if I want to change the world I must begin with myself.

> *No love that in a family dwells,*
> *No carolling in frosty air,*
> *Nor all the steeple shaking bells*
> *Can with this simple truth compare:*
> *That God was man in Palestine*
> *And lives today in Bread and Wine.*

John Betjeman

A NATIVITY PLAY W ITH A DIFFERECE

Most nativity plays over-sentimentalise the theme of Christmas. After all it's a children's feast with little to say to us adults. Little baby Jesus, sweetly sleeping in His Crib, is no great threat to any of us or the values we live by in our adult world. Yet when we celebrate the birthday of an important man or woman we do not focus on baby images but rather on the significant events of that person's adult life and what these events say to us. So we need to let an adult Christ speak to us at Christmas and to examine our conscience in the light of His message. A priest tells of a nativity play performed in his parish in a black township in South Africa which stirred his imagination with its original approach. Invited to attend he agreed out of courtesy, prepared to be bored to death but was soon surprised. Fr. Gerard Fitzsimons tells the story.

The opening scenes were along the usual lines. In act two when I saw three figures approaching I immediately thought that they were the Wise Men from the East. But no, these had come and gone for I saw their presents lying conspicuously near the Crib. The newcomers were three strange characters. One was dressed in rags and hobbled along with the aid of a stick. The second was wearing a tattered pair of shorts and was bound in chains. The third was most weird. He had a whitened face and wore an unkempt grey wig and was making strange gestures. They were certainly no wise men or kings.

As they approached, the chorus of men and women sang out, "Close the door, Joseph, they are thieves and vagabonds coming to steal all we have." But Joseph said, "Everybody has a right to this Child, the poor, the rich, the sad, the happy, the trustworthy and the untrustworthy. We cannot keep this Child to ourselves alone. Let them enter."

The men entered, bowed and remained staring at the Child. After a while Joseph took the initiative and picked up the presents the wise men had left. To the first man he said, "You are poor. Take this gold and buy yourself some food, clothes and a place to sleep. I have a trade. We will not go hungry. I do not need it."

To the second he said, "You are in chains and I don't know how to release you. Take this myrrh. It will help to heal your wounds and the chaffing in your wrists and ankles."

To the third he said, "I don't know the source of your strange behaviour and mental anguish but take this frankincense. Perhaps the smell will help to soothe your troubled spirit." At this point, the choir again sang out, "Look at him. He is giving away everything that was meant for the Child. He has no right to do that."

Then the first man addressed Joseph, "Do not give me this gift. Look at me. Anyone who finds me with gold will think that I have stolen it and beat me up." The second man said, "Do not give me this ointment. I am used to these chains. I am strong because of them. Keep it for this Child because one day He will wear our chains." The third man said, "I am lost. I have no faith. In the country of the mind I have lost faith in God and man. Will this incense cure my doubts and fears? Incense will never bring me back to the God I have lost."

While Joseph and Mary covered their faces the three men bowed and addressed the Child. "Little Child, you are not from the country of gold and frankincense. You belong to the country of want and disease and doubt. You belong to our world. We want to share these things with you."

The first, taking off his ragged shirt said, "Take my shirt because one day they will rip your garments off you and you will walk naked. Remember my gift to you then." The second man said, "I put one of my chains at your side. One day you will be led out in chains but on that day you will undo the chains of many people." The third man said, "I bow before you. Take away my doubts, my depression, my loss of faith in God and man. I am not able to carry them alone. They are unbearably heavy. I know you will help me and when you grow up you will take them all before the throne of God and bring light to my darkness."

The three now bow and walk away slowly with an upright and confident gait. Then the director comes on and explains, "The three men now go away like people who have been relieved of a heavy burden. They know they have found someone who shares their burdens and who brings them strength and courage. They go away full of hope and joy. You and I can feel the same courage, freedom and happiness here with the Babe of Bethlehem."

The parish priest, Fr. Fitzsimons, gives his final reflection. "The script was written by a man from Central Africa. I thought it was tremendous. For myself, I felt like a man who was expecting a plate of marshmallow and was hit in the face by a raw steak!

The man who had been dressed in rags was an altar server who always served Mass in his bare feet because he could not afford shoes. The men and women who wanted to chase him away were typical of religious people like myself who are so ready to judge by appearances. The stand of Joseph was truly memorable.

I drove home with the final words of *Journey of the Maji* by T.S. Elliot in my mind.

> *We returned to our places these kingdoms*
> *But no longer at ease here, in the old dispensation,*
> *With an alien people, clutching their gods."*

DEVOTION TO THE BLESSED EUCHARIST

St. John Paul 11 was a fervent promoter of devotion to the Blessed Eucharist. The reason is simple. He quotes one instruction: *The mystery of the Eucharist is the true centre of the Sacred Liturgy and indeed of the whole Christian life. Consequently the Church guided by the Holy Spirit constantly seeks to understand and to live the Eucharist more fully.* The Pope merely draws attention to a central tenet of our Christian faith. The celebration of the Eucharist is both the climax of our Christian life of prayer and it is the fruitful source from which our Christian life springs.

Catholic teaching on the Eucharist raises profound theological questions. However I just wish to offer a few insights which might help to enrich our understanding of this great mystery. How bread and wine become the body and blood of Christ I leave to the theologians. It is commonly called transubstantiation, the substance changing while the external appearance remains the same. For me the Eucharist is not so much a problem to be solved as a mystery to be contemplated. The *why* of the Eucharist is very simple. At Mass the bread and wine is changed into the living loving Christ so that in the reception of Holy Communion we too become the Body of Christ.

In the first centuries of Christianity there were no temples, no public places of worship, as the Christian religion was outlawed. The Christians were the temples of the Holy Spirit. The Church was the gathered community which achieved its fullest identity when they shared the Eucharist together. They recognised the presence of Christ among them both under the appearance of the consecrated bread and wine but also in the Community. This is an essential part in understanding the mystery of the Eucharist, namely the unity between the Blessed Eucharist and those who received the Sacrament. St. Augustine in the 5th century emphasised this point clearly. As he held up the Sacred Host before Holy Communion, he would call out, "This is the Body of Christ" and the whole congregation would respond, "Yes, we are". Charles de Foucauld one of the great missionaries of North Africa would spend hours of adoration before the Blessed Sacrament and then go out to serve the poorest of the poor. He saw a direct link, as he put it, between "adoring Jesus Eucharist and serving Jesus neighbour." This truth should have a profound influence on our Sunday gatherings at Mass if we only allowed it to sink in and live by it.

Jesus came on earth to establish the Kingdom of God. His message was one of universal love and reconciliation. Perhaps in the beginning He thought that the kingdom might be established by the power and beauty of His words and deeds. Gradually, however, as the forces of evil gathered against Him, it became evident that He would have to pay the ultimate price, the sacrifice of His life poured out in love and forgiveness. On that last night in Jerusalem as He gathered His Apostles for the Paschal Meal, He knew that His death was immanent. He used the meal for the institution of the Blessed Eucharist to express the meaning of His whole life and death, self-giving love for the Father and for all of us, the means by which God's kingdom would be established. The bread and the wine were the perfect symbols of what He was about to do. The breaking of the bread symbolised the breaking of his body on Calvary, the pouring of the wine, the shedding of his blood.

For the Apostles it must have been a rich and warm experience but also a profound mystery. In some ways they had no idea what it meant. Within a few hours they would all run away and Peter would deny that he knew Jesus. They began to understand the meaning of the Last Supper only in the light of the Resurrection. They would come together in a secret place. They would pray for unity as the Lord had instructed them at the Last Supper. They would ask forgiveness for their failures. One of them would recall an event from the life of Christ. Another might show the connection with a prophesy of the Old Testament. Then would come the solemn moment when one of them produced bread and wine. They would pray as they recalled the words of Jesus, *"Do this in memory of me."* They would pronounce the words of consecration, knowing that the living loving Christ was there among them. Two thousand years later Christian communities all over the world follow the same basic procedure.

The fundamental mystery of our Christian faith, the very foundation of our faith, is the Resurrection of Christ. The Christian community finds its fullest expression and identity in the celebration of the Eucharist. Belief in the Resurrection, in the Church as the Body of Christ and in the Eucharist are fundamentally one and the same thing. The Resurrection gives meaning to the other two. It also implies faith in the Holy Spirit which is simply the power of God released among us by the glorification of Jesus. In the Holy Eucharist we share the divine life of Christ just as He shared our humanity.

PRAYING THE DRAMA OF THE MASS

After Mass at the Shrine in Lourdes on one occasion, a lady told me that she had counted the number of priests who had concelebrated, well over a hundred and then asked me if she had attended over a hundred Masses that morning. It may be a common misconception and I pointed out to her that there is only one Mass, the Sacrifice of Christ on Calvary and that there is only one priest, Jesus the Christ. We all share in His priesthood, ordained ministers in a special way to preside at the celebration but all the baptised are a priestly people. The Holy Mass is the offering of the whole people of God. Members of the congregation are not just spectators attending Mass. They are partakers united together with the priest in offering the Holy Sacrifice. It follows that the best form of participation is to follow the prayers and the readings and to be united with the celebrant as he leads us in this supreme act of worship.

Senior citizens well remember that when they learned their catechism they were told that if they were in time for the Offertory they were in time for Mass. The penitential rite at the beginning and the readings, all in Latin, were often rattled off at speed. Devout people often said the Rosary during Mass and not many went to Holy Communion. The obligation was to attend, just to be present. Undoubtedly the great faith of countless good people such as my own parents carried them through a lack of understanding of the nature of the Mass. However there was great need for a renewal of the liturgy which was undertaken at the Second Vatican Council.

The document on the liturgy emphasised that the Mass is a community celebration, led by the priest. It is appropriate that the celebrant faces the people and invites active participation. We worship not just as individuals but as a community. This community aspect is shown throughout the celebration. We come together at the beginning in an act of reconciliation. We listen to the word of God as a believing community. The sign of peace to our neighbour confirms this. The climax comes in sharing the Bread of Life together in Holy Communion.

I like to think of the Holy Mass as a great drama in three acts. The first act is the Penitential Rite. Our Lord Himself reminds us that if we come to the altar to offer our gift and there remember that we have offended our brother or sister, we should first go and ask for forgiveness. The Penitential Rite focuses on the need for reconciliation. This word sums up the whole ministry of Jesus. He came to reconcile us all to one another and to offer us as a family of faith and love to the Father.

The second act of the drama is the Liturgy of the Word. The Council documents remind us that when Sacred Scripture is read in church, it is Jesus Himself speaking to us. Recently among Catholics there has been a great renewal of interest in Sacred Scripture but we still have a long way to go. The sacred texts are read out to us at Mass and we listen as a community. The readings are meant to guide our spiritual journey in the days and weeks ahead. The Council documents tell us that "the people of God is formed in the first place by the word of the living God." The task of the one who preaches is to make these readings relevant to the lives of the congregation, to break the sacred texts and make them inspirational and nourishing for the people just as later in the Mass he will break the Sacred Host before distributing Holy Communion. The privilege of reading sacred scripture at Mass should not be taken lightly and requires careful preparation.

The third act in this great drama is the Liturgy of the Eucharist. Beginning with the Offertory there follows the Preface, a great hymn of praise and thanksgiving. The central prayer is the Canon of the Mass leading to the Consecration and the great doxology. Then follows the *Our Father* preparing us for the incredible privilege of receiving Holy Communion, the Bread of Life, spiritual food for our earthly pilgrimage,

At the Offertory we prayed that we may come to share in the divinity of Christ just as He has shared our humanity. In Holy Communion we are united to Christ in a most intimate way. We are the Body of Christ.

THE EUCHARIST: SACRAMENT OF
UNITY AND COMMUNITY

There is a beautiful story about St. Maria Goretti or rather about the young man who murdered her. She was attacked at her home in 1902 and gave her life protecting her chastity against the lustful advances of Allesandro, a young man from the locality. She later died in hospital having publicly forgiven her attacker. Allesandro later repented, helped no doubt by the prayers of Maria. After serving his long prison sentence he was released. Coming back to his village was a real challenge for him. What would the people think? What about Maria's mother still living in the home place? Should he go back at all? The local priest helped him. In fact he took him along to visit Maria's mother, Assunta, who was prepared for his arrival, welcomed him and declared her forgiveness. In a fitting conclusion, the parish priest asked them to kneel together at Mass the following Sunday. At Holy Communion, he held up the Sacred Host and intoned, "This is the lamb of God who takes away the sins of the world..." Then he broke the Sacred Host and gave one part to Assunta and the other to Allesandro. In this Holy Communion the awful crime of murder was put behind them for good. Receiving the Sacrament together celebrated love, forgiveness, reconciliation, union with God and union with each other.

The decree on the liturgy at the Second Vatican Council had a profound effect on the way we understand the Mass. It is the offering of the whole people of God together with the priest. The people are not just spectators; they are partakers. Mass is said in the local language, with the priest facing the people to form a community. At Holy Communion there is a special bond between all who share the Blessed Eucharist. On special occasions when I say a House Mass for a family it is easy to emphasise this aspect. In a large church with a scattered congregation it is more difficult to bring out this community aspect and people need to be reminded that we are all family members united around the altar. Yet it is sadly possible for members to receive Holy Communion together and later treat one another with total coldness and indifference. I have known people to attend the same church regularly and receive the Sacraments and yet treat one another with cold hostility. This is a contradiction of what the Eucharist is all about.

The meal aspect of the Eucharist was important in the early Church. Mass was known as the *Breaking of Bread.* Because of certain abuses referred to by St. Paul in his first letter to the Corinthians, the meal element was gradually diminished to a symbolic breaking of the large host before Holy Communion. However the Eucharist is a meal as well as a sacrifice, two aspects of the one great reality.

The inexhaustible richness of this sacrament is expressed in the different names we give it. Eucharist means it is an action of Thanksgiving to God. It is called *The Lord's Supper,* the memorial of Christ's passion, death and resurrection. It also anticipates the Wedding Feast of the Lamb in the Heavenly Jerusalem. In our rich Catholic understanding of the Mass there are three dimensions, past, present and future. It is a commemoration of the passion, death and resurrection of Jesus. It makes present to us here and now the power of the Risen Christ. It is also a preparation for the future coming of Christ in glory. This understanding is captured in a lovely acclamation which we used to say after the Consecration, *Christ has died, Christ is Risen, Christ will come again.*

When we receive Holy Communion we are united in a special way, not only to Christ, but also to all our brothers and sisters who share the same Sacrament. We are all now the Body of Christ and this has strong implications for us. Let me quote St. John Chrysostom, one of the early doctors of the Church:

> *"Do you wish to honour the Body of Christ? Do not ignore him when he is naked. Do not pay him homage in the temple clad in silk only to neglect him outside when he is cold and ill-clad. He who said, "This is my body" is the same who said, "You saw me hungry and you gave me no food." And "Whatever you did to the least of my brothers, you did it to me." What good is it if the Eucharistic Table is overloaded with golden chalices when your brother is dying of hunger? Start by satisfying his hunger and then with what is left you may adorn the altar as well."*

This is strong language challenging us to realise that our social responsibilities go hand in hand with our devotion to the Blessed Eucharist. We must be as much a Christian in the home and in the market place, when we are at work or leisure as when we kneel in church on Sunday. In fact the dismissal at the end of Mass gives us this message, "Our celebration is ended; let us go forth to love and serve the Lord and each other." Strengthened by Word and Sacrament we go forth to live the Gospel message in our daily lives.

PRAYER FLOWING FROM
THE CELEBRATION OF THE EUCHARIST

The Eucharist is the summit and source of all our spirituality. The faith we profess at the celebration of Mass has to be lived out in our daily lives. The Christian witness we give during the week in our family, social and business lives, is a more accurate guide to our real faith than any nice formula of our belief, such as the Nicene Creed, which we recite each Sunday. There has to be a consistency between believing and doing. Otherwise we are hypocrites. Your life may be the only book some people ever read about Jesus Christ.

I would now like you to reflect on the words used in the Gospels leading up to the institution of the Blessed Eucharist. The sequence describing the action of Jesus is as follows: He took, He blessed, He broke; He gave. I find it fruitful in prayer to reflect on these words and apply them to myself as I try to lead a Eucharistic life.

God took me at my birth. I often ponder on the mystery of creation and the miracle of life. Out of millions of possibilities, I was created. God chose me. He has carved my name on the palm of His hand. I am unique. Whatever my personal gifts or lack of them I have something to contribute to my world that no one else can give. The spirituality of true self-esteem has nothing to do with great qualities and accomplishments. It is about accepting myself as a unique part of God's creation. All of us should walk tall. We dare to say, *Abba, Father.* We have a part to play in the building up of God's Kingdom.

God has blessed me in so many ways. By baptism, each of us was incorporated into the Church, Body of Christ. We have a right to hear God say to us individually: "This is my beloved daughter; this is my beloved son." What a privilege. Then we can reflect on the wider blessings of life, different for each one of us, but many shared in common, such as loving parents, a happy home-life, health, education, friends, the choice of career. Every day I thank God for the gift of my Christian faith and the living out of that Faith in my call to the priesthood. Some people are perhaps more aware of the negatives in their lives. Yet, it is sound advice to count your blessings one by one and give God thanks for them.

The third action in the sequence is He broke. Yes, we are all broken in one way or another. The bread for the Eucharist is baked in fire; the wine matures not on a sunny shelf but in a damp, dark cellar. In my pilgrim journey through life it is inevitable that I too experience the struggle of growing up, coping with tragedies, with the pain of parting, the death of parents and close friends, ill health, misunderstandings, failures and temptations, what Shakespeare called "the slings and arrows of outrageous fortune." Yet any crisis in my life is also an opportunity for growth. Growing old is a particular challenge for all of us. It can also be a period, not only of letting go but of letting grow. We have more time for prayer and reflection, to get our priorities right, to appreciate the kindness of others, to grow a little in wisdom and integrity.

He gave...

As Christians we are called to love and to serve. Broken and purified by the challenges of life, I should now be more prepared to be given to others in the saving liturgy of everyday life. I think of the inspiring words of Blessed Mother Theresa of Calcutta to her sisters: "Let the people eat you up."

The more available we are to others, the more some people will demand of us. The temptation is to hide away and avoid them. The Christian way is to give ourselves completely. Jesus was a man for others. We are His disciples and however inadequately we must follow his example. We are a Eucharistic people and should be willing to be broken and given. For the Eucharist to bear fruit in our lives, we have to be broken, broken by love to bring life to others, finally broken by death to bring eternal life to ourselves.

> I sought my God,
> My God I could not see.
> I sought my soul,
> My soul eluded me.
> I sought my brother
> And I found all three.

PRAYING FOR REPENTANCE

The very first words of Jesus in St. Mark's Gospel are: *"Repent and believe the Good News"*. A paraphrase of these words could read: "Be changed people for God is at work in your lives." Each time we come together for the celebration of Mass the first step is to reflect on our lives and to ask forgiveness for any faults and failings, for things I have done or things I have failed to do. The call to repentance is a constant challenge on our pilgrim journey through life. What does it really mean?

Repentance in the ordinary sense means to express sorrow for any bad deed done or evil intention, to make amends and to begin again. The Latin word for repentance is *metanoia*, which means to change course, turn around and face a new direction. But there is a deeper Biblical meaning, which entails asking forgiveness for not living up to my potential, failure to use my God-given talents for the good of the community, "things I have failed to do." Ladislaus Boros in his book *The Moment of Truth* gives us an imaginative picture of the last judgement when my real self will be judged not by the Lord, but by my ideal self, the sort of person I would have become if I had cooperated with all God's graces during life.

Plato once described the human person as a chariot pulled by two horses, one called REASON and the other called PASSION. Whichever one dominates determines the sort of person we are at a given moment. We are often shocked by the evil around us.

How can people do such things? The great Russian writer, Solzhenitzyn, who experienced so much evil in the labour camps in Siberia, once said that the line between good and evil runs through every human heart. We could say that within every man there is a hero and a scoundrel, and within every woman there is an angel and, let's say, a flawed angel! We could put it this way: Within each of us there are two souls, a little soul and a great soul. On any given day we tend to identify with one or the other. I am a very different person depending on which soul is reigning within me.

If the little soul is reigning, I may feel bitter and angry. I'm petty and afraid. I give way to hurts. I nurse a sense of grievance. I'm a bit paranoid. Everybody is against me. If the great soul, the nobler one, takes charge, when I let that reign, I'm a different person, open, compassionate, understanding of the other, willing to share, to shoulder the burden of life without complaint. I'm brave, generous and capable of heroism. Most of us I'm sure can recall both moods in our experience of life, times when we wanted to lash out and times when we could embrace the whole world.

When Jesus asks us to repent, He is thinking not only of the bad things we may have done but is asking us to identify with the great soul within us, to cease identifying with the petty soul. He's simply telling us to GROW UP, to achieve our real greatness, to move beyond our narrow vision, our present mindset. When we look at His many miracles one sees much more than a physical cure. Eyes are opened to spiritual values, ears are opened to listen to another voice. Very often Jesus does not say: *"I have healed you,"* but, *"your faith has made you whole,"* meaning you have got in touch with your great soul, that noble side of you, that side which is created in the image and likeness of God. *"Arise, get up and walk. Get in touch with your own nobility. Do not be afraid. I am with you."*

We all had moments in life when we were taken out of ourselves in a sense, when we experienced something great and beautiful and wonderful which touched us profoundly, moments of ecstasy. It may be a glimpse of the beauty of nature, a sunrise or sunset. It could be a chance encounter with an old friend, looking at the face of a child, gazing into the eyes of the beloved. I once stood on the summit of Mt. Kilimanjaro at the dawn of day and watched the sun rise seemingly out of the Indian Ocean. What an experience. There is a beautiful scene in the film "The Shawshank Redemption". Andy, the prisoner, who had just got access to some classical records, locks himself up in the warden's office, switches on the public address system and plays a beautiful aria from Mozart's "The Marriage of Figaro." The music soared above the prison compound for all the prisoners to hear. Andy's friend, Red, describes the occasion.

"I have no idea to this day what those two Italian ladies were singing about. Truth is, I don't want to know. Some things are better left unsaid. I'd like to think they were singing about something so beautiful it can't be expressed in words and makes the heart ache because of it. I tell you those voices soared higher and farther than anybody in a grey place dares to dream. It was as if some beautiful bird flapped into our drab little cage and made those walls dissolve away. And for the briefest of moments every last man in Shawshank felt free. "

In many ways we are enabled to get in touch with the divine within us. We are capable of embracing the world. Let us not forget that we have the capacity to bring out the best (and the worst) in each other. The opening words of St. Mark's Gospel are a challenge to all of us, " *Repent and believe the Good News.*" Be changed people because God is at work in your lives.

FORGIVE US OUR SINS

One of the great consolations of our Christian faith is that whatever sin we may have committed, no matter how great, if we turn to God in humble repentance and with a sincere purpose of amendment, God always forgives us. The God we worship is a God of infinite love and mercy. Those qualities became incarnate in the person of Jesus. The parable of the Prodigal Son, (Luke 15: 11-32), the return of the sinner to his forgiving father, is one of the loveliest stories ever told. In a way it is a summary of St. Luke's Gospel.

The prayer for forgiveness is the one petition in the *Our Father* with a condition attached to it. Forgive us our sins as we forgive those who sin against us. Only in the measure that we open our minds and hearts in forgiveness to others can God enter into our minds and hearts to forgive and heal us.

To forgive can be quite a challenge for people who have been deeply hurt. People who have seen members of their families killed or injured deliberately can, with some justification ask, "how can I forgive the ones who have done this?" Even when we are offended in a relatively minor way, we can be resentful and unwilling to forgive. We often tend to hold on to grudges from past offences, real or imaginary.

The Test of Discipleship
The grace to forgive others is a special gift from God which we should ask for again and again. If one were asked to list the

essential qualities of being a genuine follower of Christ, the following immediately come to mind: to be a person of moral integrity with care for justice and compassion for the poor and to worship together in community with a grateful heart. All these points are important but the ultimate test goes deeper. Jesus declares, *"But I say to you who are listening, love your enemies, do good to those who hate you, bless those who curse you, pray for those who abuse you."* (Luke 6: 27). He is telling his disciples that their virtue must go deeper than that of the Scribes and Pharisees, many of whom were good living people.

However, loving an enemy, forgiving a murderer, blessing those who curse you, this was totally outside their understanding of the law. It is what places the teaching of Jesus on such a high moral level. Such an attitude is beyond our natural powers. It is a gift of God's grace which we must pray for. Jesus gave ultimate witness to this teaching on Calvary when He prayed for the very people who planned and carried out His execution, *"Father, forgive them, for they know not what they do."*

Fortunately we have many inspiring examples of this deeply Christian response to injustice. Gordon Wilson was at the War Memorial in Enniskillen on Remembrance Sunday in 1987 when the IRA detonated a bomb which claimed the lives of eleven people, including that of his beloved daughter, Marie. Rather than being destroyed by bitterness and hatred, he publicly forgave the killers and devoted the rest of his life to bringing peace and reconciliation to the troubled province.

Another striking example was the subject of a BBC programme some time ago. It was called *Forgiving Dr. Mengele*. This was the notorious doctor who used prisoners at Auschwitz as guinea pigs upon whom to conduct the most hideous of experiments. One victim was a ten year old Jewish girl Eva Kora Together with her twin sister, Miriam, they were spared the gas chambers to be used in these experiments, such as being injected with germs and chemicals just to see the medical reaction. They suffered dreadfully but they had a strong will to live and fortunately liberation came just in time. An old photo shows two wide-eyed little girls surrounded by barbed wire fences walking out of the camp hand-in-hand on the day of liberation.

The Gift of Freedom
The little girls were taken to Canada. Coping with the problems of growing up in a new environment and the tensions of adolescence, Eva instinctively knew that while she had escaped from Mengele he still had the power to destroy her emotionally. In later life she told us, "I had two choices. I could bend and become a victim or I could forgive and claim my power back. I gave myself the gift of freedom."

Her forgiveness did not involve forgetting. She allowed herself to feel the full fury of hate for what had happened to her and others knowing that this was a healthy part of the recovery process, but healthy only if she could learn to let go, forgive and be free. Years later on a trip to Poland she was saddened to find many other survivors who were unable to share her ability to forgive. They were still victims of Auschwitz, trapped in a prison of anger and bitterness. Only late last year (2015) I read that Eva had travelled to Germany to attend the trial of a Nazi Auschwitz guard just to express her own personal forgiveness for the man on trial.

Eva is an inspiring example to all of us, especially in her emotional and psychological courage. The late Pope Paul VI wrote, "A love of reconciliation is not weakness or cowardice. It demands courage, nobility, generosity, sometimes heroism, an overcoming of oneself rather than one's adversary." One is reminded of the words of Albert Schweitzer, "The greatest force you can use against anybody is to love them."

To forgive does not imply that justice should not take place and that the process of the law should not proceed. No, justice should be seen to be done. Forgiveness is about one's personal attitude. Forgiveness is a choice we make, not a feeling. Otherwise we continue to wallow in a sea of bitterness.

Most of us, thank God, have never been the victims of grave crime. Yet some people have problems of letting go of minor hurts and misunderstandings of the past. One sees that in relatives or neighbours not speaking to each other because of some minor incident of the past. Life can be tough at times and inevitably most of us suffer. I remember a professor addressing a group of priests, religious, laymen and women, mostly teachers, and giving them this advice, "Always pray to God for the grace to forgive your parents and teachers for all the hurt they may have done you, in the hope that one day, your children and students will be able to forgive you for the harm and hurt you may do to them." He was challenging them to face up to the real world in which it is sometimes impossible to avoid misunderstandings and offences, real or imaginary. Sadly some people cling on to past hurts and keep up petty grudges and resentments. At times they may be willing to bury the hatchet, but they carefully mark the spot where it is buried! We pray for the grace to let go and forgive just as we ask God to forgive us. In that way we can be truly free.

Finally we should all avail of the beautiful Sacrament of Reconciliation We should use it regularly to experience the joy of God's mercy to all of us.

He who fails to forgive has already broken down the bridge he himself must cross. (Swahili proverb)

REFLECTIONS ON PAIN AND SUFFERING

Many books have been written on the problem of pain and suffering but in many ways it remains a mystery. When one suffers because of evil done it is understandable but what about all the suffering of innocent people? The faces of poor suffering children caught up in a war situation will always haunt us. There is no easy answer.

One of the wisdom books of the Old Testament tackles the question of why bad things happen to good people. Job is a good man, successful and wealthy. But it's easy to be good when everything goes well. Then he is afflicted with loss of property and health. His so-called comforters claim, "You must have done wrong. That is why God punishes you." Even his wife turns against him telling him to curse God and die. Job holds out but in the end he too begins to complain. Why O Lord, why? Then from the heart of the tempest God gave Job his answer: (Job 38: 1 ff)

"Who is this obscuring my designs with his empty-headed words?
Brace yourself like a fighter.
Now it is my turn to ask questions and yours to inform me.
Where were you when I laid the earth's foundations?
Tell me since you are so well informed.
Who decided the dimensions of it, do you know?
Or who stretched the measuring line across it?
What supports its pillars at their bases?

Who laid its cornerstone when all the stars of heaven were singing with joy and the sons of God in chorus were chanting praise? Who pent up the seas behind closed doors, when it leapt tumultuous out of the womb, when I wrapt it in a robe of mist and made the black clouds its swaddling bands, when I marked the bounds it was not to cross and made it fast with a bolted gate?
"Come thus far." I said "and no farther,
Here your proud waves shall break."

This beautiful passage is an invitation to ponder the mystery of creation, of time and eternity. Our planet, seemingly vast, is but a speck of dust in the incredible universe. The individual man or woman is so tiny, so helpless, yet is so wonderful, so precious in the eyes of the Creator. Job's reply is ours too when faced with the mystery of life: *"My words have been foolish; what can I reply? I had better lay my finger on my lips and listen."*

For us Christians all suffering takes on a new meaning in the shadow of the Cross. At one level Calvary was a great offence to God, the unjust suffering and death of an innocent man. Yet it was the occasion of our redemption because the sufferings and pain were accepted by Jesus in love and His life was poured out in love for us. As Jesus yields up His spirit, He can announce with calm certainty that his work is done. The final proclamation "It is finished" is not a cry of failure but the majestic cry of love's final victory.

If Jesus had not come on earth to suffer and die for us, it would be possible for a human being to do something outside the range of God, namely to suffer and die for a friend. We could say that God does not know what it is like to suffer. But the

Incarnation means that God knows his creation from the inside. When we are tempted to complain, what have I done to deserve this, we look at the Cross and ask what has He done to deserve Calvary?

There are all sorts of pain in our lives, physical, emotional, mental and spiritual. Pain can have different effects on us. It can make us self-centred and unsociable and miserable. But it can also liberate us from unselfishness, draw us away from foolish pursuits and bring out untapped resources of heroism and courage. It can make us more compassionate and caring for all who suffer. Victor Frankl once said that you can bear anything if it has meaning, and Jesus on Good Friday gives meaning to all pain and suffering. It is a good practice to include a prayer in the morning offering all our pains and sufferings to be united with those of Jesus and His Blessed Mother for the salvation of the world.

Life has sometimes been compared to a game of cards. We cannot change the hand that has been dealt to us but it depends on ourselves how we play it. For those who suffer it is well to remember that:

> **Courage is a greater gift than health.**
> **Patience can outlast pain.**
> **Love can grow stronger as the body grows weaker.**

PRAYER BEFORE THE CROSS

We celebrate the Exaltation of the Holy Cross annually on 14th September. It is an occasion to reflect not just on the triumph of the Cross but on the mystery of suffering and death as the price of victory. Although today the Cross as a symbol is sometimes hijacked by pop idols and minor celebrities as a piece of costume jewellery, it still remains the most powerful religious symbol of all. Its two simple beams are a reminder of the two great commandments of our religion. The vertical beam points to our adoration and love of God. The horizontal beam reminds us that our love of God must be reflected in our love and service of our brothers and sisters.

We should not forget the origin of the cross. At the time of Jesus, crucifixion was a common form of execution by the Romans and the cross was the symbol of death, cruelty and disgrace. After an execution the cross would be either burned or buried just as we might dispose of the soiled blood-stained bandages of a violent death victim. What accounts for the complete turn around in the meaning of the cross?

The mother of all battles was fought not in Iraq or Europe but on Calvary. There it seems that all the evil of this world, political and religious corruption, hatred, spite, mob violence and brutality, was hurled at the person of Jesus and seemed to triumph by burying for ever in Sheol the incarnation of all goodness. But no, on Easter Sunday morning, that tomb burst forth, giving new life and hope to the world. He is Risen, Alleluia. Touched by the person of Christ, the cross came to represent the triumph of life over death, of good over evil, a symbol that love is stronger than hatred, that light conquers darkness and hope prevails over despair.

Pain and suffering are an integral part of our earthly journey. Life is a mystery. We often wonder why some people have such heavy crosses to bear and why God allows this or that tragedy to happen. Above all we ask why sometimes bad things happen to good people. There is no easy answer but in meditating on the events of Calvary we get a pointer to meaning. The passion of Jesus does not glorify suffering. The story acknowledges the fear, the emptiness, the loneliness of the darkest hour. Jesus accepts the suffering as the inevitable consequence of a life of total self-giving, a life poured out in love for sinful humanity. He embraces the darkness with so much love that night becomes day.

Einstein was once quoted as saying that what we perceive as light is but the shadow of God. If so, perhaps what we perceive as darkness is the face of God. Calvary was surely the darknest moment in human history. It was also the greatest revelation God has ever given as to who He really is: total love. As we stand in silent awe before the Cross of Christ we realise that there is a power in darkness which we must understand as there is a power in silence which is the preferred language of adoration.

Down the centuries the cross has inspired successive generations to reach out in compassion and care for others and to alleviate suffering. It has given us inspiration to face our own crosses bravely and to unite them to the sufferings of our beloved Saviour for the salvation of the world.

Undoubtedly suffering can bring us closer to God. Meditation on Calvary can give us the courage to face the trials of life with faith and love. To be truly free we must be God's captive. We must be willing to surrender to God's loving care. Archbishop Fulton Sheen in an address he gave back in 1940 quoted a beautiful poem which sums up this point.

I slipped His fingers, I escaped His feet.
I ran and hid for Him I feared to meet.
One day I passed Him fettered to a tree.
He turned His head and looked and beckoned me.

Neither by strength nor speed could He prevail.
Each hand and foot was pinioned by a nail.
He could not run and clasp me if He tried,
But with His gaze He bade me reach his side.

"For pity's sake", thought I, " I'll set you free".
" No, hold this cross," He said, "and follow me.
This yoke is easy, this burden light,
Not hard or grievous if you wear it right."

So did I follow Him, who could not move,
An uncaught captive in the hands of Love.

CALVARY THROUGH THE EYES OF MARY

I am Mary, mother of Jesus, standing at the foot of the cross on Calvary. I am torn with grief and pain. Who can understand the depths of a mother's sorrow at the death of her son? But the death of this son, my son, Jesus, crucified as a common criminal between two thieves, fills me with a grief that is overwhelming and almost unbearable. I am so grateful for the support of Mary, the Apostle John and Mary of Magdala. I hardly dare to look up. I just bow my head in a torment of distress. I am united with all mothers who must watch helplessly as their sons suffer and die.

Even at this terrible time my mind goes back to the early days, days of hope and joy. Yet I had been warned. At His presentation in the Temple, on that beautiful morning, amid the many congratulations the old man, Simeon, had spoken directly to me, "A sword will pierce your own soul too". Was what is happening now the fulfilment of his prophesy?

Among the joys of young motherhood, that was forgotten. True enough there were moments that made Joseph and me think more deeply about the future. One such occasion was at his *Bar Mitzvah* in Jerusalem when he was twelve years old. After the exciting festivities, he was missing for three days and when we found him, he didn't seem to understand the worry he caused us. His statement then pointed to a deeper relationship with his heavenly Father, one that might cost him dearly.

There was another occasion which happened when he was in his late teens. I had sent him to Sopphoris to get some provisions for the house and Joseph needed a new tool for the carpentry shop. I didn't know that the Romans had crushed a local rebellion with utmost cruelty and had left the victims hanging on their crosses. On his journey my son saw all those mangled bodies. That night I heard a cry of distress from his small bedroom so I looked in. He was kneeling in prayer, intense, distraught, oblivious of all else. I heard his words, "Father, Thy Kingdom come. There is another way to all this violence. It is the way of forgiveness and love. I offer my whole life to bring about your kingdom of justice, peace and love."

There was that memorable day when he preached his first sermon in our synagogue in Nazareth. Reading from the prophet Isaiah He spoke of opening the eyes of the blind, setting the downtrodden free, bringing good news of salvation for all people. Surely, I thought then, the power and beauty of his message will be enough to win over the whole world.

He began with high hopes, gathered many disciples and we felt that a new age had come. I followed him whenever I could and was so proud to hear stories of His healing powers and the hope and comfort he gave to so many people. He was acclaimed by the crowds. What mother would not be proud of that? But strangely he often spoke of suffering and death.

When he set off for Jerusalem for this his third Passover, he seemed more preoccupied than ever. His disciples too seemed to have some premonition of trouble ahead. I told him I would travel later with another caravan. We were delayed and had just got to the outskirts of Jerusalem when the tragic news reached us. Jesus had been arrested on Thursday night and after a mock trial on Friday morning had been condemned to death and his execution was to follow immediately. He was already being conducted to Calvary.

The road to Calvary was long and steep. I tried to get near Jesus but the mob pushed me back. At one point I did manage to see him crushed under the weight of the cross. We exchanged glances. My heart was breaking to see him suffer. We struggled to reach Calvary. John was trying to help me. He appealed to the centurion in charge who made way for us to move forward but already my Son was being nailed to the Cross. I stood there with bowed head. There was jeering and curses all round me but even in turmoil of the moment I heard my Son call my name "Woman," he said, "behold your son."

Even then in that painful moment I was struck by his use of that title "Woman." He had often called me by many intimate titles for mother. But this was a different title of richer, deeper meaning. He had used it once before at the marriage feast in Cana of Galilee when I had asked him to solve a local problem. "Woman, my hour has not yet come." It attributed to me a wider role, a richer sense of motherhood in God's plan of salvation. Jesus now looked at John, a disciple close to His heart and said, "behold your mother" and at that moment I felt John's protective arm around my shoulder, and even in this hour of desolation I knew I would be cared for and I felt called to be a mother to all my Son's disciples.

The sky is now dark. There is thunder and lightening but I'm in deep shock. I hear his voice again asking forgiveness for all and then ultimately the words, "Father into Thy hands I commend my spirit." In a strange way I understood that his life's work had been accomplished and that we are all drawn into the great mystery of salvation. Yes, I too, willingly offer my Son on Calvary and my whole life for the salvation of the world.

At the Cross her vigil keeping
Mary stood in sorrow weeping
When her son was crucified.

CALVARY AS SEEN THROUGH THE EYES OF THE CENTURION

I am Antonius Longinus, a Roman centurion. I am proud of my military record, having played my part in bringing *'Pax Romana'* to various parts of the Roman empire. We centurions are respected men in charge of a hundred soldiers. True enough some of our men are rough and brutal but we can discipline and mould them into shape. I was surprised to be sent to this part of the empire, Palestine, a god-forsaken little province where nothing ever happens.

I was enjoying my stay at the seaside town of Joppa when I got a sudden order. I was drafted into Jerusalem where they were expecting some sort of trouble there around Passover, this Jewish festival which seems to bring all sorts of mischief makers to town.

When I got the call at least I had one hope. I might be able to meet the famous Jewish rabbi, Jesus of Nazareth. Rabbis on the whole don't impress me but I'm told this man is different. In fact a colleague, the centurion Claudius, told me that he had actually met him and that his life was changed for ever. Apparently one of his servants was on the point of death. Doctors had given up hope. Then someone told him that Jesus, the great healer was nearby. He rushed out and told Jesus of his servant's illness. Jesus looked at Claudius and said, "I will come and heal him". But at that moment Claudius was captivated by an incredible presence, a sense of goodness and power. He, a proud Roman centurion, found himself on his knees. He said simply, "Master, I am not worthy that you should enter into my house. I know what authority is all about and I know that if you will just say the word my servant will be healed." That was all. Jesus seemed to marvel at his faith. He even quoted it as an example to the bystanders. Claudius bowed and left knowing that his servant would be healed. And he was at that same hour. His last words to me were, "You must see Jesus. He will change your life."

See Jesus? By all the pagan gods of Rome was I destined to see Jesus. When I got to Jerusalem it was Friday morning and an urgent message awaited me. There were three men condemned to death. I was to take a detail of soldiers and see that the executions were carried out and to watch out for trouble. "Who are they?" I asked "and what have they done?" I was told, "a couple of thieves and one false prophet the religious leaders want to get rid of, a certain Jesus of Nazareth". Jesus of Nazareth! I was struck dumb. There must be a mistake. But what could I do? I'm a soldier. I must obey orders. Disobeying was not an option. Another would be drafted in to take my place, probably angry and more brutal because of the late call-up. Perhaps this I could do, yes, do my job but in doing it, I could mitigate some of the brutality that usually accompanies such occasions. Yes, I would do that.

When I saw Jesus being led forth my heart sank. But I had a job to do. It was difficult enough trying to keep the crowds back. I'm used to violence. I've been in tough spots but this was different, religious violence, even the religious leaders, the so-called holy men, were there. No, they were not in the front but hanging around the back as they urged the mob on, jeering and mocking. I was stunned. What could I do?

I saw the condition of Jesus stumbling along under the heavy beam and about to fall. I looked around. At the edge of the crowd, there was a tall muscular man. He was not jeering, just looking on out of idle curiosity. I grabbed him. "Hey you, carry that cross behind Jesus and bear the brunt of it too. I'm watching you." He was shocked and tried to run away but my soldiers stopped him. He reluctantly lifted the heavy beam. Jesus looked at him lovingly, grateful for the help. I couldn't help noticing that after a bit, Simon – that was his name – seemed to shift the weight of the beam more and more onto his own shoulder, so that by the time we reached the place of execution, he was carrying it almost completely. He even seemed reluctant to move way till ordered to do so by one of the soldiers.

There were some women there being pushed aside by the crowd. I asked who they were. One of them was Mary, the mother of Jesus. She had tried to move closer but couldn't. I made a passage and brought the women forward. By this time the cross was upright. Mary looked at me. I'll never forget that gaze of pain and anguish but also of compassion. She must have guessed that I too was suffering in my own way. I said simply, "Lady, I'm sorry. Move as close as you wish. No one will disturb you."

I felt good about my little acts of kindness amid all the brutality. But suddenly I was racked with pain and guilt. There was a long wait. The crowd bayed for blood and death but death was slow in coming. Then came darkness, thunder and lightening. But this was nothing compared with the darkness and turmoil within my own soul, the guilt I felt, the evil things I had done in the name of Rome and power and greed. I felt lost. Could I ever be forgiven and have peace? I looked up. Jesus was in agony but even then He caught my eye. Then with a sweep of his gaze, He seemed to take in the soldiers, the crowd, the chief priests, everybody, but He seemed to look directly at me as He spoke, "Father, forgive them for they know not what they do."

I don't know how long I remained there, pondering, overwhelmed by the whole event. I heard him speak other words to his mother and to another member of the family. Then came the final spasm of agony, a prayer commending Himself to His Father and it was all over. I was stunned. A hush seemed to descend on the crowd and in that moment I seemed to sense something, an overwhelming insight as to who Jesus was. I had to give voice to what my heart understood. I unsheathed my sword and lifted it high in a Roman salute and I cried aloud for all the world to hear, "Indeed, this was the Son of God."

We adore you, O Christ, and we praise you
Because by your holy Cross, you have redeemed the world.

SIMON OF CYRENE: MY DARKEST DAY TRANSFORMED

My name is Simon and I come from Cyrene. I'm a devout Jew and I always come to Jerusalem for the Passover Festival. I have two sons, Alexander and Rufus, but they are too young to travel with me so they stay at home with their mother.

When I reached Jerusalem yesterday the place was in turmoil. Last Sunday, Jesus of Nazareth had entered the city in triumph. Some say he is the promised Messiah. Certainly the zealots were trying to enlist him in their support, if not, at least to use his presence to stir up trouble. The authorities are alert to these things. They have already arrested their leader, Barabbas and they plan to have him crucified without delay.

I'm told that Jesus has also been arrested. I had often heard of him and longed to meet him. Among the religious leaders he is not accepted but the ordinary people flock to him. His teaching seems to be new, vibrant and touches the heart, a message of hope and joy and love, not the tired old litany of ritual purifications. It makes sense to me. Nobody seems to be outside the embrace of his love. He has been known to dine with tax collectors, and even prostitutes have been converted by his message of love and forgiveness.

I had longed to hear him speak. I waited all morning expecting him to be released. Then the shock came. He is condemned. The Roman Governor has given permission for his execution even though he had pronounced him innocent. My God, what is happening in our country?

I was saddened by all this but then I have never met Jesus so I cannot judge. What will I do now? It's near midday. There's tension all round so I'll leave the city for a while. Then suddenly I'm caught up in a rushing mob. "Golgotha, Golgotha," they shouted, "that's where they will be executed." I'm a bit sickened by it all but strangely led on by a weird curiosity, I found myself at the edge of a huge crowd. I was carried along by the fury of the moment, up the hill, up towards Golgotha.

Soon I had had enough and I decided to leave. Just as I was trying to extricate myself from the mob, a soldier grabbed me. "Here you, the centurion wants you," he said. He gave me a violent push. The centurion gave a curt order, "See that man; take his cross and help him to carry it. No refusal. I'm watching you."

Carry the cross! Who is this Roman? To touch the cross is a curse. I've done nothing wrong. Why me? I'll be disgraced for the rest of my life, cursed forever, reckoned as a criminal. Carry the cross, never. I dive for cover and try to escape but the crowd laugh and jeer and force me back. The centurion towers over me. "Do what I told you," he said, but then in a softer voice which only I could hear he added, "You won't regret it."

I take the heavy beam. Jesus turns and looks at me. He was about to stumble and I sort of prevented the beam from crushing him. He said nothing but looked into my eyes with a look of tenderness and compassion. I will never forget that look. I became oblivious of all else, the shouting, the jeering, the mob violence. I was only aware of the person of Jesus beside me.

I seemed to be caught up in a great drama of life, of good and evil, of love and hatred. In that flood-lit centre stage there was one person, Jesus. I reached for the heavy beam and took the whole weight of it on my shoulders.

Soon we were there. I was quickly pushed aside by the soldiers. But even then Jesus acknowledged me. He reached out and touched my cheek with his hand and uttered one word SHALOM. (Peace). I then understood that amid all the brutality and evil, that love is stronger than hatred, that light conquers darkness and that helping Jesus to carry His cross was the most privileged act of my life.

We think that Paradise and Calvary,
*   Christ's cross and Adam's tree, stood in one place.*
Look Lord and find both Adams met in me.
*   As the first Adam's sweat surrounds my face*
May the last Adam's blood my soul embrace.

John Donne.

MEETING CHRIST IN THE WOUNDED

In chapter 20 of John's Gospel we are told the delightful story of the doubting Thomas. When the Risen Saviour appeared to the other Apostles, Thomas was not with them and when they told him that they had seen the Lord, he refused to believe. The others might be suffering from illusions but not Thomas, a down-to-earth practical man. "Unless I see the holes the nails made in his hands and can put my finger into the holes they made and unless I can put my hand into his side, I refuse to believe." Then eight days later the Lord appeared to the disciples again with Thomas present. Jesus invited Thomas to touch his wounds even to put his hand into his wounded side. "Doubt no longer but believe." Then Thomas uttered his beautiful profession of faith: "My Lord and my God." And our Lord's final injunction: "Blessed are those who have not seen and yet believe."

This episode is related to strengthen our faith in the Risen Christ. The incredulity of Thomas helps us more than the credulity of the women and the other apostles. The tough minded, no-nonsense Thomas was not looking for signs of splendour, only the wounds of Christ. In John's Gospel, the Cross of Jesus and the glory of the Resurrection are two sides of the one reality. Paul saw Christ in glory. Thomas was converted by the wounds of the Cross.

Today's world likes to point to the spectacular, the splendour, the record-breaker. But more people are brought to Christ by the touching of His wounds. Blessed Mother Teresa discovered Christ in the wounds of the poor of Calcutta, Jean Vanier in the wounds of the handicapped, Oscar Romero and Martin Luther King in the wounds of their people inflicted by discrimination and injustice.

Pope Francis reminds us that we are all sinners in need of purification from our many failings and sins. Just as St. Francis of Assisi once embraced the leper, we embrace the leper within ourselves when we accept our faults and frailty in humble confession and meet the merciful Christ. We embrace the leper in our brothers and sisters when we accept them in their shortcomings, embrace them and forgive them.

Thomas made his famous profession of faith after he had touched the wounds of Christ. His search for the wounded Jesus brought him to the Christ of glory. In John's Gospel the recognition in faith of Christ's divinity is linked to the touching of His wounds. As the prophet Isaiah had foretold, "By His wounds we are healed."

When Oscar Wilde was condemned to prison he was in despair and misery. From being a great celebrity he was now a despised, rejected man. He captures the mood in one of his poems "E Tenebris" (Out of darkness).

> *"The wine of life is spilt upon the sand,*
> *My heart is as some famine-murdered land*
> *Whence all good things have perished utterly".*

He fears the wrath of God, even hell-fire itself. What saved him and brought him peace and reconciliation was the wounded hands and the face of Christ crucified.

> *"Nay, peace, I shall behold before the night,*
> *The feet of brass, the robe more white than snow,*
> *The wounded hands, the weary human face."*

In the weary, human, battered face of Christ, Wilde saw the mercy of God which drew him out of his despair and fear and brought him to forgiveness and peace.

LENT: A TIME OF SPIRITUAL RENEWAL

Jesus spent forty days of prayer and fasting in the desert to prepare for His public ministry. The season of Lent celebrates this time and directs that it should be a fitting preparation for the great feast of Easter. In the past the Church was very strict in laying down rules of fasting and penance during Lent. It was a rather gloomy season which we were glad to get through. The Church continues to emphasise the need for penance, reminding us of the words of Jesus: *"If anyone will come after me, let him deny himself, take up his cross daily and follow me."* The emphasis today is more on renewal and growth in one's spiritual life. Lent comes in springtime, a time of new life and the pruning away of the obstacles which hinder that growth.

The nature of the penance we undertake for Lent depends on our personal circumstances. We need first to look at our responsibilities and duties in life and ensure that we are living up to them. This is more important than multiplying bodily acts of penance. However it is customary to give up things for Lent and this is to be encouraged. Lent is a time for conversion and the first thing to give up is any sinful behaviour. No amount of bodily penance can compensate for ignoring sin in our lives.

However it is good to give up things for Lent, to proclaim one's mastery over such things as drink or tobacco, to cut down one's indulgence in food or TV. I think it's great for young people to give up sweets or sugar for Lent. In an age of self-indulgence they are strengthening their moral will-power and building the foundation of a good character. A river always takes the line of least resistance and usually ends up crooked. While a winding river may be a pleasant sight, a person who always takes the line of least resistance by way of indulging in anything he fancies can often end up crooked too, and this is not something to be admired.

Lent means far more than a time for giving up things. The three traditional practices put before us by the Church are prayer, fasting and almsgiving. We all need to get away at times from the many distractions of our daily activities. There are many opportunities for a weekend retreat. Even if we can't get away, we can always create a little desert experience of our own, a day or a long afternoon away from it all. We can find a quiet place for a few hours, no paper, no phone, no radio or TV, no distracting voices, just a time to be alone. Except that we are not alone. God will fill the space if you allow Him. We will become more deeply aware of His presence in our lives which is of the essence of prayer. We all need to create a time of deep listening to God in prayer, when He can reveal to us the areas in our life that need renewal. The whole purpose of the exercise is not to get away from reality but to see reality in its proper perspective, to get our priorities right, to demolish a few idols that might have crept into our lives. This enables us to plunge back into the heart of life with a clearer vision and renewed vigour.

Fasting and almsgiving are often linked together. When we realise the terrible poverty in some countries it should inspire us to deny ourselves certain luxuries in order to donate generously towards charities, whether local or national. Such organisations as MISSIO, the A.P.F. and Cafod, Trocaire and Concern in

Ireland, SCIAF in Scotland, depend on the generosity of so many people who continue to donate year after year. The contributions are often doubled during Lent which is a sign of the generosity of so many people. "Live simply so that other people might simply live" is a challenging slogan which invites us all to fasting and almsgiving.

EASTER: THE FEAST OF THE RESURRECTION

This Feast celebrates the fundamental mystery of our Christian Faith, namely that Jesus Christ, the Son of God, who shared our humanity here on earth and suffered and died on the Cross on Good Friday rose from the dead on Easter Sunday morning. His Resurrection is our guarantee that through faith in Christ we are all called to eternal life. As the liturgy puts it,

> *In Him a new age has dawned.*
> *The long reign of sin is ended.*
> *A broken world has been renewed*
> *and man is once again made whole.*

Easter celebrates an historic event, the Rising of Christ from the dead and a present reality, the continuing saving work of Christ in the world of today, through His teaching, through Mass and the Sacraments.

Easter, Ascension and Pentecost are essentially one and the same Feast, celebrating Christ's rising from the dead, His exaltation at the Father's right hand and the sending of the Holy Spirit into our lives, continuing the work of redemption. The Roman calendar tells us, "The fifty days between Easter and Pentecost are celebrated as one Feast day, sometimes called The Great Sunday." To emphasise this fact the Sundays between Easter and Pentecost are known as Sundays of Easter, not Sundays after Easter.

Easter is a season of joy. Alleluia, Christ is Risen. It is an anticipation of the joy of God's Kingdom. On many occasions Jesus referred to the Kingdom of God as a wedding feast, so Easter is the foretaste of "what eye hath not seen nor ear heard." The first Easter took place at the Jewish feast of Passover, celebrating the liberation of their people from the slavery of Egypt. We celebrate our liberation from sin and death by Christ. Baptism plays a dominant role in our lives. We too have passed through the waters of baptism to new life in Christ. Our Easter joy is not the joy of the foolish who try to pretend that problems do not exist but the joy of people who can see beyond the troubles of this life, who can shoulder their crosses because they know they have a meaning and they can see things in the light of eternity.

Did the Resurrection really happen? Was it not all just an illusion, the fantasy of a few misguided followers who wanted to prolong the dream? Is it not too good to be true? We would be less than human if sometimes we are not assailed by doubt. Yet the facts are extraordinary. The very witnesses to the Risen Christ were the disciples most of whom had run away at the arrest of Jesus. They had nothing to gain by their witness other than persecution and death. Many of them were unlettered fishermen and housewives who took on the might of the religious establishment of the day, and the power of the Roman Empire, and prevailed.

There is a beautiful scene in a play by John Masefield. It concerns Pilate's wife. Troubled because of her husband's part in condemning Jesus, she comes to the tomb on Easter Sunday morning. There is confusion all round. She goes up to the centurion still on guard and points to the empty tomb and asks,

"Is he there?" He answers, "No Madam. He is not there." She then cries out, "Then where is he?" The centurion replies, "Released into the whole world where neither Jew nor Roman can stop the power of His love."

None of the Evangelists describe the emergence of Jesus from the tomb. They are suggesting a mystery rather than reporting a news event. All the witnesses of the first Easter are unanimous about the empty tomb. Of course that proves nothing. The various accounts of the apparitions of Jesus are a summary of the shared experiences of the disciples over a period of time. They all invite us to faith in the Resurrection of Jesus who is now beyond the power of death and is the source of new life for all who believe in Him.

Christians are challenged to live their daily lives in the light of the Resurrection. We do so every time we rise above our hurts and hatreds and learn to forgive others. We do so whenever we conquer our selfishness and greed and reach out to others in their need. We do so every time we treat all our brothers and sisters with genuine Christian love.

IS MY FAITH A PERSONAL EXPERIENCE OF GOD IN MY LIFE?

Faith is my response to divine revelation as contained in Sacred Scripture. Do I look upon revelation as communication or communion? If I look upon the sacred text as God's way of communicating to me what I must believe, how I must behave and how I should worship then my response is: I believe in God, I act according to His commandments and I worship regularly. However I can also see the text of Sacred Scripture in a deeper light, as communion with God, as God sharing His life with me and my response then is an experience of love, joy and peace.

Our faith in a personal God is not just intellectual assent to divine revelation. It means total trust in God, an experience of a living relationship with a God who loves me and to whom I respond with the utmost humility and love. This relationship is nurtured by personal prayer, allowing myself to be embraced in the arms of divine providence. Of course some may have a winter experience of faith when prayer becomes dry and God seems far away. This is often God's way of testing me and of deepening my faith. It is important to persevere. Many saints relate how they experienced the dark night of the soul.

Modern research is revealing new wonders of the vast universe of which we are part. The fact that I can have a relationship with the Divine Creator of it all, Whom I can call

Abba, Father, is almost incredible. Scripture tells us that He has carved my name on the palm of His hand. I can only respond with love, adoration and thanksgiving.

From the earliest times the Creator has guided our steps and showed us how to live out our relationship with God and our neighbour. The prophet Micah (Ch 8: 6) sums it up beautifully, **"This is what Yahweh asks of you, only this, to act justly, to love tenderly and that you walk humbly with your God."**

Love is at the heart of our Christian religion. Our love for a personal God must always translate itself into love and service of our brothers and sisters. I like the word 'tenderly' because love requires gentleness and respect. In walking humbly with our God we are deeply aware of our own faults and failings. In loving tenderly we accept the faults and failings of others. We are willing to listen and to be a healing presence to them. Love is not just a sentimental feeling. It is a deliberate act of the will in responding to others whether they are attractive to us or not. It is the most powerful force for good in dealing with both friends and enemies, as Jesus reminds us again and again. This love is often expressed in forgiveness and reconciliation. In this year of mercy we realise that mercy and forgiveness are both expressions of love.

The prophet reminds us to act justly. This implies not only honest living and treating others fairly but it urges us to play our part in promoting social justice and to speak out against any discrimination against the weaker members of our society and to try to remove structures of injustice if these exist. Our missionaries, supported by the A.P.F. have played an important role in highlighting and removing injustice in many countries.

LET MARY THE VALIANT WOMAN BE OUR INSPIRATION

Devotion to Our Lady has always been an integral part of our rich Catholic tradition. As a young lad growing up in rural Ireland I recall that the family Rosary was common practice in most households. In those far-off pre-TV days sometime between supper and bedtime my mother would round up the family. Visiting neighbours would join in and she would lead us all in saying the Rosary.

We took our decade in turn, hoped we had counted right when it came to the Gloria; then at the end we waited patiently while she got through all the 'trimmings,' the extra prayers, when all the needs of the family and parish were put before the Lord. Though we were often reluctant participants at the time, down the arches of the years I can still hear the soft cadence of my mother's voice as she led us on and I bless her memory.

The mysteries of the Rosary are a summary of the great mysteries of our religion, the birth, life, passion, death and resurrection of Christ, Our Saviour. The very repetition of the Hail Mary is almost a mantra leading us into contemplation. The Rosary remains one of the most beautiful ways of honouring Mary and bringing us closer to Jesus.

Devotion to Mary has helped people in many ways. At a time when Church teaching in general was rather stern, with a lot of emphasis on sin and sanctions and God presented as a rather exacting judge, the face of the Mother of Jesus helped to soften the picture. And when times were tough we always prayed to Our Lady for help. There is an old Irish saying which translates as, "God is strong and He has a good mother."

What was Mary like? Too often she is depicted as other-worldly, meek and mild, not really part of our messy, broken world. Nothing could be farther from the truth. In a telling passage from *Marialis Cultus,* a document on Mary, the late Pope Paul VI writes, "Mary was anything but passive and submissive, pious to the point of being out of contact with reality. No, here was a woman who did not hesitate to assert that God is the avenger of the oppressed, that He topples the mighty of this world from their thrones. In Mary we recognise the valiant woman, who has known poverty and suffering, flight and exile." No wonder we can pray to her in all our needs for she too lived through the storm and stress of the human condition.

It's important to have a proper understanding of Mary within the mystery of Christ and the Church. This matter was keenly debated at the Second Vatican Council. It touches on the mystery of the whole process of salvation which was a fundamental issue of the Reformation. We believe that Christ is the one mediator of salvation but He chooses not to be alone in the work of mediating the saving love of the Father. He associates with Himself, His Body, the Church, seen both as institution with sacraments and hierarchy and as the People of God, the communion of saints. The people of God continue His saving work and Mary is not only the chief member but also the figure, the Mother, the model of what a Christian is called to be.

Pope Paul VI outlined four points which should underline all devotion to Mary.

a)   Mary was a woman of faith. She was so open to God's call; her faith was so strong that she became the rainbow which spanned heaven and earth, which enabled the Word of God, as it were, to float down and pitch His tent among us. Mary is the inspiration for each of us to discern God's will and faithfully follow it.

b)   Mary responded to God's call with praise and thanksgiving. Her beautiful hymn of praise begins, "My soul glorifies the Lord." Too often our prayers are limited to petitions rather than to praise and thanksgiving for all God's goodness to us. Each of us, however inadequate we feel, can write our own *Magnificat* because the Lord can do great things for us and through us.

c)   Mary brought forth the Word in fruitfulness. Through her Jesus became present to Joseph, the shepherds, the poor, the lowly, to the world at large. Our vocation too is to make Jesus present in the world we live in by the witness we give to the Christian faith we profess. My life may be the only book some people read about Jesus Christ. What do they read there?

d)   Mary offered the Word in sorrow on Calvary. Mary, the valiant woman, stands beside us in times of tragedy and sorrow. She gives comfort and consolation to all who mourn. She is a source of strength to all who suffer for she too stood at the foot of the Cross.

All our devotions to Mary, whether private rosaries or simple prayers, public devotions or pilgrimages to the great Marian Shrines, lead us to a deeper love of Jesus our Saviour and to a greater fidelity to our Christian vocation. May Mary, Mother of the Church, pray for us all and may she be our inspiration, our joy and our courage as we continue our earthly pilgrimage.

MATER DEI

When Gabriel brought his message.
I've sometimes heard it said,
You took the road he showed you,
Knowing little where it led.

> *God would not ask this of you,*
> *No blinkered way you trod.*
> *Naught was hidden from you*
> *For you knew the mind of God.*

I read it in holy book
That the coming of your boy
Brought with it no birthing pains,
But an ecstasy of joy.

> *No mystic epidural*
> *Was acceptable to you*
> *So you suffered in his coming*
> *As myriad mothers do.*

I heard a parish priest to say
And a pious man was he,
That you swooned away in grief
As He hung upon the tree.

You were braver far than that
And you stuck it to the end,
Though the final tortured twitch
Through your soul a sword did send.

When Ascension Day was over
By then, 'tis said, you'd gone
To middle-class retirement
In the household of St. John.

Not so, you ever laboured
For the glory of the Three,
For such is your vocation
Through all eternity.

Anon.

USING SACRED SCRIPTURE FOR PRAYER

Lectio divina is used frequently today as a method of prayer. It means sacred reading or a prayerful reading of Sacred Scripture. The word of God in Jewish tradition had two meanings. Firstly it was a message of God relayed to the people by one of the prophets. Secondly it was a significant event, the interpretation of which was a powerful message from God. Thus God spoke to the people through the Exodus from Egypt or the Babylonian captivity, through a success or a failure. They saw the finger of God in all such events.

For Christians the Word of God has a wonderful third meaning. The Word became flesh and dwelt among us. Jesus is God's ultimate word of love to us and He is our word of love back to the Father. Thus Jesus is the perfect mediator. Our relationship with Jesus is the foundation and heart of prayer.

Lectio divina is simply prayerful reading of Sacred Scripture, allowing God to speak to us through the reading. This challenges us to respond to God's word in the light of the reading and in the context of our present circumstances.

Obviously some parts of Sacred Scripture are more conducive to prayer than others. The Bible is really a library of books, some historical, some prophetic, some are wisdom books. The four Gospels of the New Testament are the heart of the Bible. These are four portraits of Jesus and the Christ event. They were written not to give biographical details or to satisfy human curiosity but in the words of the evangelist, St. John, *"These are recorded so that you may believe that Jesus is the Christ, the Son of*

God, and that believing this, you may have life through His name."
(John 20:31). The four Gospels are most commonly used for *lectio divina* but many other parts of Sacred Scripture are also very suitable.

Let us now look at the simple process of *lectio divina* using a passage from St. Mark's Gospel, chapter 6, verses 45 to 52. There are four stages involved. We first read the passage which tells the story of how Jesus came walking on the water to his frightened disciples in the storm tossed boat and how He calmed the sea and their fears. We read the passage a few times and imagine the scene. Then we meditate on the text and see the significant aspects. When Mark wrote this some thirty years after the death of Jesus, Christians were being persecuted badly. They were in the storm tossed barque of Peter and many were losing heart. Jesus seemed so far away. The evangelist recalls this event from the ministry of Jesus and the message He gave to the disciples, "Courage. It is I. Do not be afraid."

The third part of *lectio divina* is talking to God about the significance of these words to my life today and the life of the Church. We too are going through critical times. The fourth watch represents the darkest period of the night when our spirits are at their lowest ebb. Many Christians today are feeling the strain. In our modern secular world religion may not be persecuted but is often treated as irrelevant and this is often harder to take. We have declining congregations, fewer religious vocations and the deep pain of clerical scandals. Is it any wonder that our faith in the Divine Presence of Jesus is being tested? Many are confused and disheartened by what is happening. In prayer I can express my confusion and anguish, my pain and concern, my hopes and fears. I bring them all to God. Then I move to the fourth stage of *lectio divina*.

This is called contemplation or simply listening to God in love and adoration, opening my mind and heart to the presence of a loving God. What is He saying to me through the challenges facing me? What does he want me to do? The bottom line of all prayer is to discern the will of God and do it. Jesus speaks to me as He spoke to His disciples, "Courage. It is I. Do not be afraid." Faith is tested in times of trial.

The four stages of *lectio divina* are reading the text, meditating on it, talking to God about it and then listening to what God is saying to me. These stages often intermingle but our prayer should always end with a period of contemplation, a loving awareness of God in my life, letting God's love embrace me and give me the courage to face the challenges that lie ahead.

Gradually we get a deeper understanding of Sacred Scripture as a light for my life and a source of inspiration. The letter to the Hebrews tells us that the Word of God is alive and active and it cuts like a double-edged sword. We are consoled and healed by it but also challenged and even disturbed by it. We must not avoid passages in Sacred Scripture which challenge us but let them speak to the heart. If we are disturbed by such passages this may be a grace from God inviting us to spiritual renewal. God will always give us the graces we need.

THE PSALMS: TREASURE FOR ALL SEASONS

The Book of Psalms, containing 150 in all, is the basic prayer book of the Jewish people. The psalms were written over several hundred years and reflect many events in the glorious and often tragic history of the Jewish people. They have power to stir the human heart as no other literature can do. Every human emotion and aspiration seems to be contained in the psalms, whether of joy or sorrow, love, hope, fear or regret. They represent humankind's eternal search for God and for meaning in our pilgrimage through life.

The different authors were close to the people and could identify with all their experiences. They shared all the ups and downs of life, tried to give meaning to all events and faced the most difficult question, why do bad things happen to good people. Their written words were put to music to be sung in Temple worship. Inspired by God, the psalms are a unique collection of prayers.

The book of psalms was used by the Jews both in their public worship of God in the Temple and in private prayer. Jesus would have learned the psalms at his mother's knee. They would have been recited at family prayer and He would have sung them with fellow worshippers in the synagogue. At the Last Supper He and His disciples would have recited the Hallel (Psalms 112 -117) recalling the liberation of their ancestors from the slavery of Egypt and their fidelity to the worship of the one true God, the Glorious and the Merciful.

We are all familiar with the cry of Jesus on the Cross, *"My God, my God, why hast Thou forsaken me?"* It comes from the beginning of Ps. 22. It is not a cry of despair because psalms have to be taken in their entirety and this one ends on a note of triumph, "All the nations of the earth shall bow down before God."

Our Lord made the psalms His own and they became part of the prayer of the early Church. They are used extensively in today's liturgy especially in the Mass and in the Prayer of the Church, usually called the Divine Office which priests and religious say daily. Happily today more lay people are joining in praying the Divine Office which is a rich treasure of spiritual inspiration. We do need to do some study on the background of some psalms to appreciate their context of origin. While some of the psalms are not suitable for us – the few imprecatory or cursing psalms are now often omitted - most of psalms are invaluable for private prayer. Many people have their own favourites which they use on special occasions and find them immensely rewarding.

An important ingredient in all worship is a sense of awe and reverence, the basis of the relationship between the creature and the Creator. The psalms go to the heart of this and remind us of the attributes of God, the all-knowing, the all-powerful, the all-merciful. They speak of God's eternal years, His unfailing mercy and His tender loving care for all his creatures, great and small.

At the beginning of a retreat I often recommend participants to ponder on Ps. 139 as it leads us into the presence of a loving God. *"It was You who created my inmost being, knit me together in my mother's womb. I thank You for the wonder of my being, for the wonders of all your creation."* (v. 13-14)

Some of the psalms speak of the promised Saviour and His future coming, His sufferings, death and resurrection. As the Jews went through long years of suffering we can imagine how they longed for the coming Messiah. As we read these psalms in hindsight we can see how beautifully they were fulfilled in Christ. They make one's study of the Gospel all the richer.

Many of the psalms deal with the malice of sin and the hard-heartedness of the sinner and then point the way to redemption Ps.51, *Miserere*, (Have mercy on me, O God) is a magnificent hymn of sorrow containing all the required dispositions for genuine repentance, including a cry to God for help and a full acknowledgement of one's sinfulness and responsibility.

The psalms provide us with a sober reminder of the passage of time and how transient all life is. There are plenty of warnings against idolatry, especially against the idols of our modern world, wealth, power, luxury, celebrity and ease. Although the psalms were written some three thousand years ago, human nature has not changed. We are in constant need of conversion, as Ps 37 reminds us:

> *Do not worry about the wicked,*
> *Do not envy those who do wrong.*
> *Quick as the grass they wither,*
> *Fading like the green of the field.*
> *Trust in Yahweh and do what is good.*
> *Make your home in the land and live in peace.*

One of the most beautiful aspects of the psalms is the way they look at nature. Ps 19 begins, *"The heavens proclaim the glory of God and the firmament shows forth the work of His hands."* The mountains are a symbol of God's majesty and power. The heavens and the stars reflect the immensity of God and the deep mystery of His being so incomprehensible and yet so attractive to our minds. As modern science probes more and more into the secrets of the vast universe it is well to ponder with love and awe the Creator of it all.

Much can be written of the beauty of the psalms. We should delve into them and taste the treasures for ourselves.

PRAYER AS CELEBRATION, NOT JUST OBLIGATION

One of my favourite definitions of prayer is a loving relationship with God. That relationship is expressed in different ways, by a life of integrity, by public worship and by the personal intimacy of private prayer. A spirit of prayer flows from my faith in a personal God. Faith is a gift of God and is my response to God's revelation. The depth and quality of faith in each of us may vary and that will greatly influence the way we pray.

Some Christians have what I call social faith. They received their faith together with their cultural background, part of the family tradition, a package they inherited. In reality it doesn't touch their lives too deeply. They are happy enough to be classed as Christians. They usually attend church at Christmas and Easter and on other special occasions but their Christianity does not influence the important decisions they make in life. Their commitment to a Christian way of life is quite shallow. For them prayer is a vague concept. In times of crisis they may turn to God but in general prayer does not figure much in their lives.

Many sincere Christians have what I call a dogmatic faith. Theirs is a firm commitment to strong belief and practice and to regular worship. It is the solid foundation on which most of us build our Christian lives. We believe, we live a life according to Christ's teaching and we worship regularly with a Christian community.

We may fail at times but we ask forgiveness and by and large we are faithful to our baptismal promises. Many good Christians live out their lives at this level and we may ask: what more is needed?

Prayer for many at this level is part of their daily lives. They are faithful to Sunday Mass, to daily prayer and to certain devotions. This is very good but sometimes one detects that their motivation is fulfilling an obligation rather than celebrating a relationship. I once asked an acquaintance of mine, a regular Mass goer, how his new parish priest was doing. His answer was enthusiastic, "Oh a great man. On Sunday morning he has us all out of Church in less than half an hour!" In other words we have fulfilled our obligation, now let's get on with the rest of the day.

Perhaps this attitude is more common than many of us would like to admit. I saw it in my own life as a priest. After ordination the duty of saying the Divine Office daily was a serious obligation. We were told that to leave out even a small section was a serious sin. This instruction kept us all very faithful to the recitation of the Office and many times after a busy day I would struggle to have it finished before midnight. But it was a chore, an obligation, a burden which I often resented. The Divine Office consists mainly of psalms from the Old Testament, psalms of praise and thanksgiving, of hope, joy and sorrow, many of them extremely beautiful. Yet I said them for years without really appreciating their beauty. It was only when I got away from the obligation idea and tried to integrate the saying of the Office into a daily routine of prayer that I began to appreciate the beauty of the psalms. Praying them now is a celebration of my relationship with a God who loves me and to whom I reach out in my human frailty. As regards Sunday Mass, of course we have an obligation to worship regularly but I much prefer the term Sunday Celebration rather than Sunday Obligation.

All this points the way to developing the third level of my Christian faith. The sincere solid dogmatic faith which we have should be deepened and enriched by a personal experiential faith. Catholics have often fought shy of talking about feelings or religious experiences. We much prefer to speak of duties and obligations. They are more clearly defined. Some Christians are a bit like the elder brother in the famous parable of the Prodigal Son as told in St. Luke's Gospel. They are faithful and fulfil all their duties but through it all remain a bit cold, distant and judgemental. They never experience the warmth of the father's embrace as the younger son did on his return. We all have a right to that embrace. Love, joy and a deep sense of peace is our birthright. This personal experiential faith gives rise to a deeper prayer life, to a loving awareness of God revealed in the Person of Jesus of Nazareth. Prayer then is not just a duty but the celebration of my relationship with a God who is my Father.

GROWING IN LOVE WITH JESUS

The foundation of our Christian spirituality is our relationship with Jesus. Our aim must always be to know Him more clearly, to love Him more dearly, to follow Him more nearly. The great Spanish mystic, St. Teresa of Avila, gives this advice: *Whether you are just a beginner or have reached the heights of mysticism, you begin and end with the humanity of Jesus Christ.*

In our theology we were taught that Jesus was truly human and truly divine. We accepted that without question. In a way it was easier to believe in the divinity of Christ than in his humanity, at least in the implications of His humanity. As divine, Jesus had all the answers, no problem. What kind of knowledge did Jesus have? He had acquired human knowledge, mystic and divine knowledge.

The implications of His humanity were not often fully realised. To be truly human is to share the human condition, to share the darkness, the doubt, the uncertainty of our pilgrim journey. Christ's awareness of His own divinity is a huge theological question. St. Paul tells us clearly: *"His state was divine, yet he did not cling to his equality with God but emptied himself to assume the condition of a slave and become as men are..."*(Phil, 2: 6-7).

The sufferings and temptations of Christ make no sense unless we accept his complete humanity, that Jesus had to cope with the darkness, the fear, the uncertainty of the human condition. It is only when accepting this, does His true greatness,

His integrity, His courage shine out in all its glory. It was when pondering deeply on the humanity of Jesus and all its implications, I can say it was only then that I truly fell in love with the person of Jesus of Nazareth.

It was also a great help to my prayer life, conscious as I was of my own distractions and inadequacies but assured that the key to success was to stay close to Jesus. There is an old painting of a powerful muscular man rowing a boat and making good progress against a strong wind and tide. His little daughter is in front of him with one tiny chubby finger barely touching the oar. The title of the picture tells the story: "Father and I are rowing." The child represents each one of us in our frailty. As long as we stay close to Jesus, the rower, He will lift all our prayers in a powerful hymn of love and praise to the Father.

The documents of the Second Vatican Council are much quoted today though it was held over fifty years ago. They called for a great spirit of renewal in our Catholic Church. The Council did not issue any specific document on Jesus, but His presence pervades all sixteen documents, especially the document on the Liturgy. This urges active participation of the faithful which includes receiving Holy Communion. This should set the faithful aflame with Christ's love. Sacred Scripture read at Mass is the power of God's word, Jesus speaking directly to our needs.

There is one passage in the document on the Liturgy, not often quoted but to me a powerful statement and consolation. It reads:

"Jesus Christ, High Priest of the New and eternal Covenant, by assuming human nature, has introduced into this earthly exile that hymn which is sung throughout all

ages in the halls of heaven. He attaches to himself the entire community of humankind and unites them with Him in singing this divine song of praise."

Here we have a vision of the Incarnate Son of God as a sort of priestly choir-master for the entire human race. It gives us a Christ-centred vision of the work of salvation. All of us are called to join him in a world wide hymn of praise to the Father. It doesn't matter if we feel inadequate, if our voices are a bit rusty, we have confidence because we belong to that choir.

When working in Uganda, I used often take a stroll at night under the clear tropical sky. Looking up into the vast universe, with the above passage in mind, it was easy to say the great doxology of the Mass: ***Through Him, with Him, in Him, in the unity of the Holy Spirit, all glory and honour is yours, almighty Father, for ever and ever. Amen.***

I began this article by quoting St. Teresa of Avila. Let me end with a quote from the great Jesuit Superior, Pedro Arupe, who when asked about Church reform said: ***"Fall in love with Jesus, stay in love with Jesus and that will decide everything. "***

THE JESUS PRAYER

St. Paul tells us in 1 Thes. 5:18, *"Pray constantly and for all things, give thanks to God, because this is what God expects you to do in Christ Jesus."* If we are called upon to pray constantly, how do we go about it? I learned the morning offering prayer at my mother's knee. "O my God, I offer Thee all my thoughts, words, actions, pains and sufferings of this day for Thy honour and glory, in union with those of Jesus Christ and of His Blessed Mother." I still say it first thing every morning and it does help to bring a great focus into whatever I do throughout the day. It is also a restraining influence on any wayward actions or attitudes I might be tempted to indulge in. You can hardly offer uncharitable words or actions or neglecting one's duties, to the honour and glory of God!

The only addition I make to the morning offering is that I include the joys and happy events of the day as well as the pains and sufferings. A long time ago, I was told by my retreat Director that the Irish are inclined to think that only painful and difficult things are meritorious in God's eyes. He was right. Such an attitude is contrary to Celtic spirituality which delights in the beauty and goodness of all creation.

My favourite definition of prayer is a loving awareness of God in my life. If we believe in the indwelling of the Blessed Trinity and that God is in the very air we breathe, this should not be too difficult. Many good men and women keep that awareness alive by the use of ejaculatory prayers throughout the day such as "Sacred Heart of Jesus, I place all my trust in Thee." Growing up in rural Ireland, I still recall that a common greeting when meeting men out in the fields ploughing or harvesting was "God bless the work." Times have changed. The pace of life is vastly different today but there is still a great thirst in the hearts of all of us for a spiritual meaning to life and the need to express it.

The Jesus Prayer provides an excellent way to pray constantly. It is most widely used in the Orthodox tradition. The words are very simple: "Lord Jesus Christ, Son of God, have mercy on me, a sinner." The history of this prayer goes back to the early centuries of the Church when short "arrow" prayers were practised. Its repetition leads to inner stillness and peace.

In the Old Testament, knowing a person's name gave one power over that person and so God would not disclose His name. But in the New Testament, Jesus tells us explicitly to call God Our Father and to have access to the Godhead through his own name. *"Hitherto, you have asked nothing in my name. Ask and you will receive that your joy may be complete."* (Jn. 16:23).

The Jesus prayer can be used by all classes of people, housewives, farmers, cab drivers, social workers, business people, teachers and pupils alike for we can all identify with sinful humanity. It is particularly suitable in times of distress or anxiety. It is very helpful to take a little time out in early morning and during the day to say it repeatedly. It can gradually become part of my whole approach to God. It can be said while driving, tidying up the room, visiting a friend, before making a decision. It is often called the Prayer of the Heart.

The words of the Jesus Prayer sum up the whole teaching of the Bible about Jesus. It is a capsule of Christian doctrine. Jesus stands for the God made man, the name under which He bore our sins and died for us. Christ is the anointed one. He is the King, the Lord of life and death, the Master under whose banner we are proud to march. Son of God points to the bridge between heaven and earth, Jesus-Saviour, Christ-King, the way into the heart of God. He is truly the Way, the Truth and the Life, to whom we gladly give worship, praise and adoration. From such a Master, it is easy to ask for forgiveness for ourselves and for the whole of humanity..

Lord Jesus Christ, Son of God, have mercy on me, a sinner.

THE SPIRIT OF THE BEATITUDES

Whenever I'm examining my conscience, perhaps at the end of the day or preparing to receive the Sacrament of Reconciliation, there is often a temptation for complacency. I'm not aware of having done anything seriously wrong. I have a few positives in my favour. I'm not such a bad chap after all! Then I measure myself against the spirit of the Beatitudes and complacency is out the door as I realise that I still have a long way to go. The Beatitudes have been described as *"the identikit of the true disciple of Christ".*

In Matthew's Gospel, chapters five, six and seven contain the essence of the teaching of Jesus. The Scripture scholar, Barclay, calls Chapter 5, verse 1-12, the Beatitudes, the essence of the essence of His teaching. Here we find the qualities of the true disciple. The introduction to Ch. 5 is important. Jesus went up the hill. This is a reference to Moses who went up Mount Sinai to receive the ten Commandments. Here is Jesus, Our Redeemer, not just accepting those commandments but inviting us to a much deeper level of commitment.

On a pilgrimage to the Holy Land, we visited the Mount of the Beatitudes and I read the text to our small group slowly and reverently. It was easy to imagine the original scene on this hill overlooking Lake Galilee, Jesus addressing His disciples with those immortal words, words which challenged the whole culture of the time and the many accepted values of that or any age.

The deep search for happiness is at the heart of every person. It is not to be satisfied by achieving power or wealth or indulging in pleasure. St. Augustine reminds us, "You have made us for yourself, O Lord, and our hearts are ever restless until they rest in Thee." The first of the Beatitudes tells us, "Blessed are the poor in Spirit" referring to those who seek happiness by trusting in God alone. Most of us like security, achievement, worldly success and that is understandable. But we need to remind ourselves that the Incarnation of Jesus was a step into total insecurity. The three temptations of Christ were all basically temptations to act from a position of power, to use His divine power to achieve His mission. He rejected them because that was not the way of salvation. "Get behind me, Satan," was His severe rebuke to Peter who had protested that the Lord should not suffer. Redemption would be accomplished by letting go of everything that we hold dear. On Calvary, stripped naked on the cross, Jesus was bereft of everything except His total trust in a loving Father. "Father into Thy hands I commend my spirit."

We need to be poor in spirit. Whatever our success in life, our material possessions, our various achievements and we should thank God for these and for all His blessings, provided we remember the great paradox of life. At the end of our days, the only treasure we will have is what we have given away, not only material gifts, but our love, our time for others, our forgiveness, our concern and kindness. All that will weigh us down at the end of our days is what we have held onto, our possessions, our pride, our ambitions, our grudges, our refusal to forgive, our many attachments to earthly values.

When Jesus proclaimed the Beatitudes, he was not speaking in abstract terms. He was thinking of the lives of His mother and foster father and I'm sure many good men and women that He knew. It has been my privilege as a priest to have known many men and women who to a greater or lesser degree embodied the spirit of the beatitudes. They are at the heart of any Christian community.

When we view he headlines of our daily papers today we see how necessary that spirit is to counteract the many false values of modern life. So when I feel challenged in reading the beatitudes, I look on that as a grace from God. At least I keep these ideals before me knowing that the only failure on my part will be to stop trying to live up to the ideal.

FURTHER REFLECTIONS ON THE BEATITUDES

The listing of the Beatitudes (Matt. Ch 5: 1-10) is one of the best known passages in Sacred Scripture. After Jesus was baptised by John, He had undergone the temptations in the desert, called his first disciples and now He began to proclaim a message of repentance because the Kingdom of God was at hand. Repent and believe the Good News. His call was: Be changed people for God is at work in your lives.

Jesus called his disciples to him. He sat down, the well known posture of a Master about to give authentic doctrine. The sermon began with the Beatitudes. The qualities outlined give a true picture of the character of the people of God. Taken together they form a portrait of the disciple of Christ. They make perfect sense only to the true disciple, one who has listened to Jesus and put on the mind of the Master.

In some English translations the word 'happy' is used instead of 'blessed' when listing the beatitudes. Neither word does full justice to the original which describes the inner joy and peace that comes from a good conscience, of knowing deep down that we are right with God. It includes a happiness that does not depend on what is happening around us, a happiness that comes to the soul being favoured by God. It is a happiness that even sickness or persecution cannot take from us.

The second beatitude is: **Blessed are those who mourn for they**

will be comforted. We note the change in tense. In the first beatitude we are told that those who are poor in spirit possess the Kingdom. Now the promise is for the future, those who mourn will be comforted. Mourning indicates the pain and sorrow which we experience over some loss such as the death of a loved one or some personal tragedy. It is part and parcel of our pilgrim journey on earth. We mourn over the many examples of sinfulness in the world around us, of man's inhumanity to man. We mourn over natural disasters such as a tsunami which claims many lives. We are sorrowful when we see children dying of hunger in a world of plenty.

It is often good to feel sorrow within ourselves and to express it, yes even to feel broken-hearted at times. Sometimes when giving retreats I challenge people with the question: When was the last time you sobbed with grief because you really cared? This beatitude gives us freedom to grieve. Mourning means to be able to let emotions surface and then give expression to them, to shed tears of sorrow and compassion. Sorrow is not an evil to be avoided. It is a process of healing as we begin to feel whole again. Jesus is our model in how to mourn. He wept over Jerusalem because of its refusal to accept Him. In the agony in the garden, His heart was broken with sorrow. The great theologian, Dietrich Bonhoeffer reflects on this:

Sorrow cannot tire us or wear us down. It cannot embitter us or cause us to break down under the strain, for we bear our sorrow in the strength of Him who bears us up, who bore the whole suffering of the world upon the cross.

The disciple can be comforted knowing that Jesus redeemed us from all evil, that through the power of that redemption, God will wipe away all tears from our eyes and death will be no more. Mourning will give way to gladness and joy. Psalm 22 tells us to be brave: *If I should walk in the valley of darkness, no evil would I fear. You are there with your crook and your staff. With these you give me comfort.*

The problem of pain is one of the mysteries of life for which there is no clear answer, especially the question of why bad things happen to good people. Why does an all powerful and merciful God allow natural tragedies to happen, such as a tsunami? From the book of Job onwards great minds have wrestled with the problem and it remains a mystery. Atheists use it as an argument against the existence of God. Our Christian faith deals with the tragedy of suffering in a very profound way. Jesus, Emmanuel, God-with-us, walked the path of pain and agony through the door of death to the glory of the Resurrection. He assures us that the tragic accident, the fatal heart attack, the tsunami, is not the end of the story. Because of the Christ event, we shall be comforted. Sadly if we take God out of the picture, the tragedy is the end of the story.

Auschwitz 2004

"Where was God?" the woman asked
At Auschwitz in the driving snow.
Around us in the air there hung
The screams of sixty years ago.

I looked at Christ upon the Cross,
Hanging, twitching, throbbing, raw,
"Where was God?" I asked myself,
And then I saw.

Anon

MORE ON THE BEATITUDES

Blessed are the meek is the third beatitude. In modern language meekness often indicates weakness and docility but in the Bible the meek are those who have a spirit of self-control and gentleness. Moses, the great warrior leader who freed the Jews from the slavery of Egypt, is described in the Bible as a meek and humble man. Being meek and gentle are strong characteristics. In real life there is nothing as gentle as real strength and nothing as strong as real gentleness. It is only the arrogant bully, unsure of himself, who tries to push his weight around. We should always pray for a spirit of humility and meekness.

The fourth beatitude praises **those who hunger and thirst for righteousness.** Hunger and thirst refer to the deepest needs of the human person and cry out for satisfaction. That strong yearning should reflect my desire to do the will of God in all situations, both in my own personal life and in my social responsibilities, in my search for social justice. Edmund Burke once said, "The only thing needed for the triumph of evil is for good men to do nothing." There is always the danger of seeing evil being perpetrated and failing to raise our voice in protest. We leave it to others, but our voices are important. Missionaries are reminded that they should not only help the poor but always combat structures of injustice which are at the root of the problem. We must always actively promote what is right and just.

Blessed are the merciful is the fifth beatitude. It is at the heart of Christ's teaching. He refers to it again and again. God's forgiveness to us is conditional on our willingness to be merciful and forgiving to others as He explicitly mentions in the great prayer He taught His disciples, the *Our Father.* Being merciful is a beautiful quality in any person. However, showing mercy and forgiveness is often the hardest thing for some people. In my priestly ministry I was often asked by people who had suffered grave injustice, "How can you forgive in such a case?" The answer is that we can do so only by the grace of God. We ponder the example of Jesus who amidst the horror and brutality of Calvary prayed, "Father forgive them." We must all ask for that grace as it is essential for the healing of our own lives.

Blessed are the pure in heart for they shall see God. This, the 6th beatitude, refers not just to the virtue of chastity but to inner purity and singleness of mind. The heart in the Bible stands for the will, the choices one makes. To be pure in heart means that our desires, our thoughts and intentions are pure and untarnished by sin and that the will is single minded and determined to be pleasing to God in all things. From those who are pure of heart come only good things, acts of love and mercy and self-sacrifice, just as our Lord reminds us that from the heart that is defiled there arises evil thoughts and impure desires, evil intentions and blasphemies. We must constantly pray, "Lord create a new heart within me, that I may see You in all things."

The 7th Beatitude is: **Blessed are the peacemakers.** God's whole redemptive plan was to reconcile mankind with God and to create unity and community here on earth. At the last Supper just before He died for us, Jesus prayed intensely for His followers, *"May they all be one, Father, may they be one in us, as you* *are in me and I am in you."* St Paul tells us that as followers of Jesus there can be no distinction between Jews and Greeks. We are all one in Christ. Our Church is a sacrament of unity and community. As we look around the world today, we see so much disunity, many factions and quarrels even among Christians themselves. We realise how vital is the role of the peacemaker and how we all should play our part in bringing peace and reconciliation wherever we can.

Blessed are those persecuted for the sake of justice, is the eighth beatitude. We have only to read the daily papers to realise how many good people are suffering today for the sake of justice. They include many Christians persecuted for their faith and countless men and women who stand up for what is right and good often at the cost of suffering and sacrifice. They inspire us and we pray for them. We should always support them within the limits of our own resources. We can always contribute to associations set up to combat injustice. We can write letters of support and make our views known. It all helps.

THE PRAYER OF CHARLES DE FOUCAULD

Charles de Foucauld who was beatified on 13th November 2005 was a most unusual man. Born in 1858 into an aristocratic French Catholic family, he lost his faith during adolescence. He joined the French military, served in Africa and was sent home in disgrace when he was discovered to have smuggled his mistress to accompany him. Later he rejoined and served with distinction. He explored many areas of Algeria and Morocco and was quite impressed by the many Muslims he met who were so dedicated to their daily prayer.

This inspired him to continue his own search for a meaning in life. On his return to Paris he was fortunate to be guided in his search by his cousin, Madame de Bondy, and by Abbe Huvelin with whom he had many discussions on religious belief. At an appropriate time, the Abbe discerned that it was time for Charles to face up to a decision. "No more discussion", he advised Charles. "What you need to do is make a good confession, return to the faith of your youth and begin again." This was a great turning point in the life of Charles. It happened in 1886 when he was 28 years of age. This was how he puts it himself, "From the moment I believed in a personal God, incarnate in Jesus Christ, I knew I had to live for Him alone."

Never one for half measures, he devoted himself to long hours of Eucharistic Adoration and serving the poor. His ambition was to imitate as closely as possible the person of Jesus.

This brought him to Nazareth, where he worked as a handyman and spent long hours of Adoration at a nearby convent. To facilitate this he had a small hermitage built next to the convent with open access to the chapel of the Blessed Sacrament.

Previously he had joined a Cistercian monastery, but considered the life there was not strict enough for him. His memories of Africa continued to haunt him. He accepted ordination, so that he could celebrate Mass and have the Blessed Sacrament with him as his plan was to return to the desert in Africa and to live as a hermit among the poorest of the poor. He settled down among the Tuareg tribe in the southern Algerian region of Tamanrasset. He built a sort of small hermitage/fort settlement. He would spend hours before the Blessed Sacrament, but his door was always open to all comers. He studied their language and culture and wrote detailed notes that are of lasting value. He envisaged forming a community who would evangelise these poor people, a community that would embody his own spirituality based on Eucharistic adoration, simplicity of lifestyle and fraternity to all, especially the poor.

Sadly in 1916 Charles was killed by a band of raiders who thought this strange Frenchman must have gold or guns hidden away in the hermitage. They got nothing. Charles' blood from a gunshot wound drained away into the desert sand. He had made no convert, his life a seeming failure. Yet some years later, inspired by his heroic life, two congregations were founded, *The Little Brothers of Jesus* and *The Little Sisters of Jesus*. They continue to this day their apostolate of presence among the poor, living a life of prayer and adoration. Also inspired by the heroic life of Bro. Charles as he was called, groups of secular priests came together in many counties to form fraternities. A fraternity usually consists of six or seven priests who commit themselves to simplicity of lifestyle, to daily adoration of the Blessed Sacrament and fraternity. They meet once a month for Gospel sharing, Review of Life and Adoration, followed by a simple meal. The fraternity has proved a great support for many secular priests who otherwise might feel a bit isolated. It provides a forum wherein one can search for Gospel values, share one's hopes and fears, failures and successes with one's fellow priests and with their help try to discern the will of God for each of us. I have found the Fraternity of enormous help and support in my own priestly life. The prayer which is said by all of us is Blessed Charles' own reflection on the *Our Father*.

It is a most challenging prayer, called **the Prayer of Abandonment:**

Father, I abandon myself into Your hands.
Do with me what You will.
Whatever You may do, I thank You.
I am ready for all, I accept all.
Let only Your will be done in me
And in all Your creatures.
I wish no more than this, O Lord.

Into Your hands I commend my soul.
I offer it to You with all the love of my heart,
For I love You Lord, and so need to give myself,
To surrender myself into Your hands,
Without reserve and with boundless confidence,
For You are my Father.

THE CELTIC WAY OF PRAYER

The great English writer and Catholic convert, G.K. Chesterton, attended the Eucharistic Congress in Dublin in 1932. Among the many happy memories of his visit which he liked to recall were two in particular. One was the singing of *Panis Angelicus* by the great Irish tenor, John McCormack, at the Congress Mass, magnificent singing deeply imbued with faith and love. The other memory was more homely. He was travelling on a Dublin tram on the eve of the Eucharistic procession and overheard two old ladies talking about it and the danger of rain spoiling the occasion. One of them said, "Of course it won't rain, Maggie, sure God doesn't want to drown Himself." Chesterton, whose ears were tuned to subtle theological arguments, was deeply touched by the woman's simple solid faith in the Real Presence of Jesus in the Blessed Eucharist.

Our Catholic faith is sacramental. It uses material things to mediate God's presence among us. Jesus used the ordinary elements of bread and wine at the last Supper to leave us a permanent memorial of His Passion, Death and Resurrection. The water of baptism mediates God's saving grace, the oil of anointing brings healing and forgiveness.

As well as using material things in a sacramental way, there is a strong symbolism in nature very much in keeping with the way the ancient Celts looked at the world. They had a great love of the natural world which for them was not just a reminder of

God but the medium through which God spoke to them. St. Patrick, who had learned a great deal about Celtic culture during his time in Ireland as a slave, did not try to wipe out their traditional beliefs. Rather he took what was best in their culture; he affirmed it and re-expressed it in terms of the Christian Gospel. A typical example of this is the Celtic Cross. Patrick told the people who were sun-worshippers that the sun was simply part of God's creation and should remind them of Christ, the Light of the World who died on the Cross for our salvation. To emphasise the point, he stamped the Cross on the sun.

The Celts stressed God's role as creator of heaven and earth and the Book of Genesis tells us that all things are good. God is at the heart of all created things. We must not see heaven and earth, soul and body, spirit and matter, as diametrically opposed. There is an intimate, essential relationship between the human, the natural and the divine. As the wellknown Irish poet Patrick Kavanagh vividly tells us, God 'is in the bits and pieces of every day.' Kavanagh (1904 – 1967) from Co. Monaghan, lived in difficult times. There was great poverty and he had a hard life on a small farm. Yet his spiritual vision shone through much of his writing. In his epic poem *The Great Hunger* describing the hardships of rural life, he goes on to say,

Yet sometimes when the sun comes through a gap,
These men know God the Father in a tree.
The Holy Spirit is the rising sap
And Christ will be the green leaves that will come
At Easter from the sealed and guarded tomb.

The essence of Celtic prayer is contained in what is known as *St. Patrick's Breastplate*. As we dress in the morning we can say,

> *I bind unto myself today*
> *The strong name of the Trinity*
> *By invocation of the same,*
> *The Three in One and One in Three.*

Facing the challenges of the day ahead we are not afraid because

> *I bind unto myself today*
> *The power of God to hold and lead,*
> *His eye to watch, His might to stay*
> *His ear to hearken to my need.*

One should read the whole prayer to reflect on its power and its beauty.

The following is part of a great Celtic blessing,

> *Deep peace of the running waves to you,*
> *Deep peace of the flowing air to you,*
> *Deep peace of the quiet earth to you,*
> *Deep peace of the Son of Peace to you.*

In Celtic understanding the God we worship is not an abstract deity but a God who by the Incarnation walked our pilgrim journey and shared our joys and sorrows. The Celtic way of prayer is to acknowledge this God at the heart of our lives and to be aware of His presence in all our activities.

> *Christ be with me, Christ within me,*
> *Christ behind me, Christ before me,*
> *Christ beside me, Christ to win me,*
> *Christ to comfort and restore me.*

One of the most beautiful poems in the English language is by Joseph Mary Plunkett (executed for his part in the 1916 rebellion). It is entitled *The Presence of God* and it captures the Celtic Christian imagination.

> *I see His blood upon the rose,*
> *And in the stars the glory of His eyes.*
> *His body gleams amid eternal snows,*
> *His tears fall from the skies.*
>
> *I see His face in every flower,*
> *The thunder and the singing of the birds*
> *Are but His voice and carven by His power*
> *Rocks are His written words.*
>
> *All pathways by His feet are worn,*
> *His strong hand stirs the ever-beating sea,*
> *His crown of thorns is twined with every thorn,*
> *His Cross is every tree.*

ASCEND TO YOUR GOLDEN YEARS. GROWING OLD GRACEFULLY

Our western culture puts great emphasis on youth, strength and bodily beauty. It is very easy for senior citizens to feel inadequate, cast aside and irrelevant in our busy modern world. They are slowing down, the best years seem to be over. There is not much ahead save declining faculties, perhaps a touch of arthritis or rheumatism and a potentially humiliating dependency on others. They can feel rather useless. Such a perspective is wrong from a Christian perspective and I hope the following words will be a source of consolation and encouragement to all who are in the evening of life.

The French have a name for our senior years. They do not call them the declining years but *'la vie montante,'* the ascending years. La Vie Montante is in fact the name of a lay Christian movement which started in Paris in the late 1950s. Men and women who were experiencing the problems of growing old came together to explore the Gospels to find some inspiration there which would help them to cope with their disabilities. The insights they found there, outlined below, became the spiritual foundation of a movement which has since spread to many countries.

Jesus did not experience old age and yet everything associated with growing old seems to have been packed into those last few days of His life which were a continuous letting go of all that we hold dear. He let go of the popular acclaim of the crowds. The cheers of Palm Sunday were changed to the jeers of Good Friday. He let go of his close disciples. most of whom ran away, one denied Him and one betrayed Him. He let go of his physical freedom and comfort not through the process of illness or ageing but by the chains, the lash and the crown of thorns.

He let go of His personal dignity. He was abused and spat upon. He seems even to have let go of His mental equilibrium by his cry of "My, God, my God, why hast Thou forsaken me?"

In the end He was bereft of all that we hold dear. Stripped, high and naked on the Cross, He was left with nothing except His total trust in a loving Father. Redemption was accomplished not by power and glory, but at the moment of His greatest weakness by a life poured out in total love and trust.

In the great drama of Calvary Jesus experienced loneliness, fear, pain and abandonment. His sufferings encompassed all the disabilities and fears that can accompany growing old. His attitude was total acceptance of His Father's will. The more we can imitate this loving attitude of Jesus in our acceptance of life's trials and crosses, the more effective and meritorious our prayers can be. The prayers of the old and sick can be very powerful if they can be poured out in union with the sufferings of Jesus for the salvation of the world.

Sometimes when giving retreats to retired missionaries and religious who might feel that their useful days were over, I would begin a conference with the words, "Now that you are entering the fullness of your Christian vocation."

Old age is a time for letting go, letting be, but also a time for letting grow. That is what La Vie Montante is all about. It is a movement full of love and joy. It doesn't deny the trials, the fears, the difficulties that are part and parcel of the ageing process, but there is a full understanding of the positive value of this stage of our lives. These are not the declining years but the golden years, the prime of an ascending life.

In our senior years we have more time to be immersed in the great mystery of God and the universe. By our Christian faith we believe that death is the gateway to eternal life which was opened for us by the death and Resurrection of Jesus. At the last Supper Jesus assures His disciples, *"Do no let your hearts be troubled. Trust in God and trust in me. There are many rooms in my Father's house. If there were not I should have told you. I am going now to prepare a place for you. And after I have gone and prepared you a place, I shall return to take you with me, so that where I am you may be too."* (John 14: 1-4)

Teilhard de Chardin, the great Jesuit priest and scholar, wrote a beautiful prayer, offering his life to God during his final years. Here is part of it:

When the signs of age begin to mark my body
(and still more when they touch my mind),
when the ill which to diminish me or carry me off
strikes from without or is born from within,
when the painful moment comes
when I am suddenly awaken to the fact
that I am ill or growing old and absolutely passive
within the hands of the great unknown forces,
grant then that it is You (provided only my faith is strong enough)
who are painfully parting the fibres of my being
in order to penetrate to the very marrow of my existence
and bear me away within Thyself.

WONDERFUL COMPANY FOR OUR FINAL JOURNEY

November is the month of the Holy Souls when we are reminded to pray especially for our dear departed ones. The communion of saints is a very enriching part of our Catholic belief, indicating that there is a special bond between those who have gone before us and ourselves, still on our earthly pilgrimage. Harvest time, the fall of the leaf, is nature's way of gently reminding us of our own mortality. It need not be such a troubling thought. In Celtic understanding, time is not a straight line which comes to an end but a circle to be completed. Death simply completes the circle, the last great moment when our life here on earth reaches its fulfilment. What is death but the blowing out of the candle because the dawn has arrived.

Death for many remains a taboo subject and a fearful thought. We take a major step in emotional maturity the day we accept our own mortality as a reality rather than as a notion, a step from notional to real assent. When we are young we are immortal. Even though we are aware of some young people dying because of illness or accident we feel that this will not happen to us. But as we grow older we are challenged to pause and reflect. There are plenty of reminders of how quickly time flies. Some things that were once so important to us now seem rather trivial. We get a different perspective on life and values. We learn from experience and grow in maturity. Psalm 38 reminds us,

O Lord, you have shown me my end
How short is the length of my days.
Now I know how fleeting is my life.
You have given me a short span of days.
My life is as nothing in your sight,
A mere breath, the man who stood so firm,
A mere shadow the man passing by
A mere breath the riches he hoards,
Not knowing who will have them.

These words are not meant to depress us but to help us get our priorities right. It is a worthy practice to pray for a happy death. We do it out of love and not out of fear. For the Christian death has a positive meaning. By our baptism we have symbolically entered the tomb with Christ and rose again to new life in Him. With St. Paul we can say, "For to me, to live is Christ and to die is gain." The Christian understanding of death receives privileged expression in the liturgy of the Church,

Lord, for your faithful people life is changed not ended.
When the body of our earthly dwelling lies in death
We gain an everlasting dwelling place in heaven.

It is natural to fear death but some good people have an inordinate dread of it. It may be a past failing or a faulty image of a vengeful God often created by misguided preachers. I have attended some people during their final days who were haunted by guilt feelings some of which were totally without any foundation. It is a privilege to be instrumental in bringing the peace of Christ to such. Even people racked with genuine guilt from past offences should not be overcome by fear but rather turn to a loving God revealed in the person of Jesus who forgave the penitent thief on Calvary. "Today you will be with me in paradise,"

St. Joseph is the patron of a happy death. Having protected both Mary and Jesus during those early years, the last mention of him is in St. Luke's Gospel (Ch.2), after the famous incident when Jesus was lost in Jerusalem when He was twelve years old. He does not appear during our Lord's public ministry and it is presumed that he had already died. There is a beautiful stained glass window in our chapel in Kilkenny, depicting Joseph on his deathbed, close to Mary and with Jesus holding his hand. What wonderful company for that last final journey. He will certainly assist all of us when our turn comes if we appeal to him in prayer.

The best preparation for a happy death is a life lived with integrity and generosity. We will be judged finally not by our wealth and achievements but by the way we have reflected Christ's love to others in our daily lives. Even if we are aware of some grave failures along the way we should not give way to fear but turn to God who is infinitely merciful and forgiving. During His life Jesus often indicated His presence by these words, "Be not afraid." At this crucial moment in our lives His words are comforting and reassuring. "Be not afraid. I have gone before you. Come follow me."

It is well to remind ourselves of the great Christian paradox, that the real treasure we will have at the end of our days is what we have given away to others, not just material things but our time, our love, our forgiveness, our visits to the poor, our words of advice and comfort. The only burden weighing us down is what we have held onto, by way of greed, unforgiving attitudes, bitterness, pride and ambition.

Prayer of Cardinal Newman for a happy death:

May God support us all day long till the shades lengthen and the evening comes and the busy world is hushed and the fever of life is over and our work is done. Then in His mercy may He give us a safe lodging and a holy rest and peace at the last.   Amen.

Prayer of Fr. Bede Jarrrett, O.P.

The souls of the just are in the hand of God.   They are at peace.
Their hope is full of immortality.   We give them back to you, O God,
Who gave them to us.   Yet as you did not lose them by giving,
So we do not lose them in their return.
Not as the world gives do You give, O Lover of souls.
What you give, You do not take away
And what is yours is ours also if we are yours
Life is unending because love is undying.   Death is only a horizon
And a horizon is nothing but the limit of our sight.
Lift us up strong Son of God that we may see further.
Cleanse our eyes that we may see more clearly.
Draw us closer to Yourself that we may see ourselves
To be closer to our loved ones who are with You.
While You prepare a place for us, prepare us also
For that happy place that where You are
We may be also for evermore.   Amen

TO BELIEVE OR NOT TO BELIEVE: CALLING MR. DAWKINS

Some time ago a friend gave me a copy of a book, *The God Delusion*, by Richard Dawkins, an Oxford professor and militant atheist, who claims that the world would be such a wonderful place if all religions were eradicated. He goes so far as to say that teaching children religion is a most evil form of child abuse. The language throughout is strident, arrogant and offensive. However the book has sold many copies in Britain and Ireland. Dawkins has been given a platform on many radio and TV shows to expound his views. He is hailed as a great prophet by fellow atheists.

However, I offer a few comments which might be helpful in putting Dawkins's thesis into a wider context. For a more detailed rebuttal I would refer the reader to a slim volume by a fellow Oxford professor and onetime atheist, Alastair McGrath, called *The Dawkins Delusion*. He neatly dismantles many of Dawkins's spurious arguments and finds many of his conclusions intellectually unsustainable.

Dawkins claim that as you cannot prove the existence of God from science that therefore God does not exist is hardly logical. He goes beyond his brief. Let me quote from an editorial by Bill Allen in *The National Geographic* some time ago. He writes,

Faith and science have at least one thing in common; both are lifelong searches for the truth. But while faith is an unshakeable belief in the unseen, science is the study of testable, observable phenomena. The two co-exist and may at times complement each other. But neither should be used to validate or invalidate the other. Scientists have no more business in questioning the existence of God than theologians had in telling Galileo that the earth was the centre of the universe."

From science you cannot prove that God exists but neither can you prove that God does not exist. One must look for a wider reference.

The fact is that many eminent scientists are firm believers in God. Isaac Newton was by common consent one of the greatest scientists that ever lived and his discoveries form the basis of modern science. This is well known but less well known is the fact that Newton was an intensely religious Christian man and his writings on religion far outstripped those on science. He once reflected, *"A little knowledge leads away from God but much knowledge leads towards Him."* That may be what one reviewer of Dawkins's book was thinking when he wrote that Dawkins's writing on God is like someone *"holding forth on biology whose only knowledge on the subject is the Book of British Birds."* (Tony Eagleton in the London Review of Books).

Dawkins and fellow atheists often use unfair and dishonest tactics in attacking religion. They tend to group together all sorts of items such as tarot cards, horoscopes, psychic phenomena and various forms of superstition with genuine religious beliefs, and that provides an easy target to demolish. They ignore the fact that genuine religion rejects all superstitious nonsense such as tarot cards and horoscopes. They often equate belief in God with religious fanaticism, suicide bombers and way out fundamentalist sects. This is dishonest because nothing hides the face of God as much as distorted religion and sadly religious beliefs can be twisted and distorted to meet evil ends. One thinks of suicide bombers who are promised ludicrous heavenly rewards if they die for Allah. Down the years terrible things have been done in the name of Christianity. It is an illustration of the dark side of human nature and how religion can be manipulated by evil people. It is not an argument against genuine belief in God.

Psychologists tell us that the most basic search in life is not for power or pleasure but a search for meaning. Our incredible human intelligence is always asking questions, reaching out beyond this visible world to try to understand the meaning of human existence. It is here that our atheistic friends are left floundering in their little cells of materialism, imprisoned by their myopic view of life. Even Bertrand Russell, the great mathematician and atheistic scientist, who derived so much pleasure from his research and teaching was pessimistic at the end. Shortly before he died he wrote a moving but sad reflection,

"No dungeon was ever constructed so dark and narrow as that in which the shadow physics of our time imprisons us, for every prisoner believed that outside his walls a free world existed. But now the prison has become the whole universe. There is darkness without and when I die there will be darkness within. There is no splendour, no vastness anywhere, only triviality for a moment and then nothing."

What a gloomy view of life, triviality for a moment and then nothing. Is that what atheists wish to promote? A character in Shakespeare's Macbeth summed it up neatly. *"Life is but a walking shadow... a tale told by an idiot, full of sound and fury, signifying nothing."* Is that all there is to life? Well most people are looking for something more, something beautiful and inspiring, a view of life that has meaning and beauty and goodness, and that's what my faith in Jesus Christ gives me. My parents shared their faith with me from my earliest days. They told me the story of Jesus and put before me high ideals of truth and goodness, kindness and generosity, love and respect for God and man, the meaning of dedication and the challenge of life, the beauty of nature and of all creation. Is that what you call child abuse, Mr. Dawkins?

I'm always amused by the efforts of some atheists to explain the prevalence of world-wide religious belief. The latest is a theory that some form of evolution has given us a religion gene to help us cope with life. We are hard-wired to believe and that both collectively and individually we are closer to belief than to disbelief. There is quite a struggle ahead for us all to overcome the religion gene and move up the evolutionary ladder to the happy world of atheism! Well, what will they think of next? If you believe that, then why not leprechauns and little green men to help us cope with life? It reminds me of Chesterton's saying that when someone loses belief in God, he doesn't believe in nothing; he believes in anything. The argument about the religion gene of course can be turned neatly upside down showing that atheists are at the lower rung of the evolutionary ladder and have a long way to go to develop the religion gene to help them search for real meaning.

Faced with the marvellous complexity of human life and the vastness of the universe, there is a deep instinct in all of us to search for a meaning behind it all. Our belief in a Supreme Being whom we call God who created and guides the universe is surely more logical than to think of the universe coming about by pure chance. If I believe the latter then I can believe that the latest jumbo-jet is the result of an explosion in a junk yard or that the magnificent paintings in the Sistine Chapel are the result of simply splashing paint at random on a ceiling or wall.

Belief in God of course does raise difficult questions. The greatest of these for me is how to reconcile my belief in a loving, all-powerful God with the presence of so much evil in the world and so much innocent suffering. I believe there will be a day of reckoning for all but I'm still left with the question of why innocent people suffer for things they have not done. Why does a loving, all-powerful God allow natural disasters such as an earthquake or a tsunami causing the deaths of thousands? There are no easy answers. Jesus, whom we believe was the Son of God, was himself the innocent victim of torture and death. He does not give me all the answers but my faith in Him helps me to live with the questions and sustains me in my darkest moments.

On one radio programme Prof. Dawkins was asked some searching questions by David Quinn who put to him, "If you're an atheist how can you believe in objective morality and free will?" Dawkins waffled a bit and then added. "I'm not interested in free will. It's not a big question for me." Quinn reminded him, "It's a vast question because we can't be considered morally responsible beings unless we have free will." Dawkins also dismissed the miracles at Lourdes as insignificant, ignoring the fact that over four thousand medical experts from all over the world have studied the records at the medical bureau at Lourdes of the many miracle cures which took place at the Shrine and many pronounced them very significant. It's hardly scientific to ignore awkward facts when they don't fit in with your conclusions.

The fundamental question of all which Dawkins and fellow atheists cannot answer is: why is there something rather than nothing?

Is Isaac's apple superseded?
And Albert's trek where no one dared?
Crooned we not as we nursed our young
That E = mc squared?
Am I a dull dim-witted dunce,
Who blindly utterly fails to see
How that which never ever was
Could up and cause itself to be?

Anon

CONCLUDING ARTICLE.

Once you accept the existence of God, however you define Him, however you explain your relationship with Him, then you are caught for ever with His presence in the centre of all things. You are also caught with the fact that man is a creature who walks in two worlds and traces upon the walls of his cave the wonders and the nightmare experiences of his spiritual pilgrimage. - **Morris West.**

The wonders and the nightmare experiences of religion are clearly painted on the walls of our modern world. We have the beauty of Christian worship and the heroic lives of countless men and women inspired by Christ. This contrasts with the atrocities and disasters perpetrated in the name of religion distorted by fanatics. The deepest question for all of us is: *what is the meaning of life?* Today many give up the search and find fulfilment in success in their careers, in sport, entertainment, whatever. The modern world provides endless distractions. Much of this can be worthwhile and good. But the basic question keeps cropping up: what's it all about, what comes at the end? We all need hope. One of the saddest features of life today is the number of suicides by people who have lost all hope.

Many in the past looked to the Catholic Church for answers. But in recent times the Church has lost a lot of credibility. Certain scandals didn't help and in general there is a strong reaction against any big institution directing our lives. Yet for all its faults the Church remains the Body of Christ. It is made up of human members with all the strengths and weaknesses that that entails. I believe that the Gospel of Christ embodied in its teaching is the key to understand the meaning of life. The truth that each man or woman is a unique creature created in the image and likeness of God, redeemed and sanctified, and destined to be united with God in heaven, gives meaning and purpose to life. The challenge for all of us is to live lives worthy of that dignity.

I have served God in the Church for over sixty years of priestly ministry. It was a fulfilling life, yet often I have been shocked and saddened by the scandals and mal practice of certain members and of the distortions made of Christ's message of hope and forgiveness. But the brighter side has always inspired me. As Fr. Rolheiser reminds us, *"The Church has produced saints, morally challenged the planet and made, however imperfectly, a house for God to dwell in on this earth. To be a member of the Church is to carry the mantle of both the worst and the finest heroism of soul... because the Church always looks exactly as it looked at the original crucifixion: God hung among thieves."*

The definition given by St. John Paul 11 has a gentler tone: *"We are a community of faith and love, confessing Jesus Christ as the Son of God and Lord of history and Redeemer and Saviour of the whole world."* Pope Francis, our present Holy Father, speaks so beautifully of the joy of the Gospel and the infinite mercy of God.

As I end these few lines I quote from my ordination card of 1955: *O God of infinite mercy, bless me in Thy service and grant that through my humble ministry many will be brought to know and love Thee.* I do hope that over the years I have helped to bring people to a vision of a God of goodness, mercy and love, a God revealed in the person of Jesus Christ, our Saviour..

PAINTED BUTTERFLIES

BY FR. CHRISTOPHER FOX, MHM

Memories of a Missionary

From the Review in The Irish Catholic

"The author is a Mill Hill priest who celebrated the Diamond Jubilee of his ordination this year. In this memoir he describes his experiences in Ireland, Britain and the U.S.A.; but the heart of the book deals with his very varied and often harrowing experiences in Africa, largely in Uganda, a country that went through years of civil war and social turmoil. But these very great difficulties were balanced by better days. "My own attitude to the many challenges of life has been one of optimism," he says. "For me the glass is always half full."

A moving addition to the growing body of Irish missionary memoir, a wonderful record of courage and witness.

Painted Butterflies
Is available in some bookshops. Price €14.95.

Also available online from
www.choicepublishing.ie
Tel: 041-9841551

And from the author:
Fr Christopher Fox, M.H.M.,
50 Orwell Park, Rathgar,
Dublin 6.Tel: 01-4127718